CCCC STUDIES IN WRITING & RHETORIC
Edited by Victor Villanueva, Washington State University

The aim of the CCCC Studies in Writing & Rhetoric (SWR) Series is to influence how we think about language in action and especially how writing gets taught at the college level. The methods of studies vary from the critical to historical to linguistic to ethnographic, and their authors draw on work in various fields that inform composition—including rhetoric, communication, education, discourse analysis, psychology, cultural studies, and literature. Their focuses are similarly diverse—ranging from individual writers and teachers, to work on classrooms and communities and curricula, to analyses of the social, political, and material contexts of writing and its teaching.

SWR was one of the first scholarly book series to focus on the teaching of writing. It was established in 1980 by the Conference on College Composition and Communication (CCCC) in order to promote research in the emerging field of writing studies. As our field has grown, the research sponsored by SWR has continued to articulate the commitment of CCCC to supporting the work of writing teachers as reflective practitioners and intellectuals.

We are eager to identify influential work in writing and rhetoric as it emerges. We thus ask authors to send us project proposals that clearly situate their work in the field and show how they aim to redirect our ongoing conversations about writing and its teaching. Proposals should include an overview of the project, a brief annotated table of contents, and a sample chapter. They should not exceed 10,000 words.

To submit a proposal, please register as an author at www.editorialmanager.com/nctebp. Once registered, follow the steps to submit a proposal (be sure to choose SWR Book Proposal from the drop-down list of article submission types).

SWR Editorial Advisory Board

Victor Villanueva, SWR Editor, Washington State University
Anna Plemons, Associate Editor, Washington State University
Frances Condon, University of Waterloo
Ellen Cushman, Northeastern University
Deborah Holdstein, Columbia College, Chicago
Asao Inoue, University of Washington, Tacoma
Jay Jordan, University of Utah
Min-Zhan Lu, University of Louisville
Paula Mathieu, Boston College
Nedra Reynolds, University of Rhode Island
Jacqueline Rhodes, Michigan State University
Eileen Schell, Syracuse University
Jody Shipka, University of Maryland, Baltimore County
Vershawn Ashanti Young, University of Waterloo

Translanguaging Outside the Academy

Negotiating Rhetoric and Healthcare in the Spanish Caribbean

Rachel Bloom-Pojar
University of Wisconsin-Milwaukee

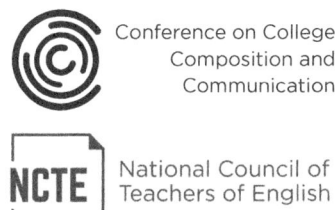

Conference on College
Composition and
Communication

National Council of
Teachers of English

Staff Editor: Bonny Graham
Manuscript Editor: JAS Group
Series Editor: Victor Villanueva
Interior Design: Mary Rohrer
Cover Design: Mary Rohrer and Lynn Weckhorst

NCTE Stock Number: 39929; eStock Number: 39936
ISBN 978-0-8141-3992-9; eISBN 978-0-8141-3993-6

Copyright © 2018 by the Conference on College Composition and Communication of the National Council of Teachers of English.

All rights reserved. No part of this publication may be reproduced or transmitted in any form or by any means, electronic or mechanical, including photocopy, or any information storage and retrieval system, without permission from the copyright holder. Printed in the United States of America.

It is the policy of NCTE in its journals and other publications to provide a forum for the open discussion of ideas concerning the content and the teaching of English and the language arts. Publicity accorded to any particular point of view does not imply endorsement by the Executive Committee, the Board of Directors, or the membership at large, except in announcements of policy, where such endorsement is clearly specified.

NCTE provides equal employment opportunity (EEO) to all staff members and applicants for employment without regard to race, color, religion, sex, national origin, age, physical, mental or perceived handicap/disability, sexual orientation including gender identity or expression, ancestry, genetic information, marital status, military status, unfavorable discharge from military service, pregnancy, citizenship status, personal appearance, matriculation or political affiliation, or any other protected status under applicable federal, state, and local laws.

Every effort has been made to provide current URLs and email addresses, but because of the rapidly changing nature of the Web, some sites and addresses may no longer be accessible.

Library of Congress Cataloging-in-Publication Data

A catalog record of this book has been requested.

For my parents, Janet and Edward Bloom. I am who I am because of you.

Also, to those who have ever felt unsure whether they or their community-based research "fit" in academia or rhetoric and writing studies, this one's for you.

CONTENTS

Acknowledgments   ix

Prologue   1
1. Toward a Rhetoric of Translanguaging   9
2. Research Design   30
3. Complicating Language Ideologies   40
4. Cultivating Translation Spaces   59
5. Contexts and Collective Resources   88
6. Critical Reinvention between Communal and Institutional Discourses   117

Conclusion: Rhetoric, Expertise, and Community Discourses of Health   129

Appendix: Interview Protocol   137
Notes   141
Translator's Note   143
Works Cited   145
Index   151
Author   157

ACKNOWLEDGMENTS

I AM ETERNALLY GRATEFUL TO ALL THE PEOPLE I worked with in the Dominican Republic, and everyone involved with the program that I refer to as El Centro para la Salud Rural (CSR) (*The Center for Rural Health*) who shared their time and knowledge to make this project a reality. Palabras no pueden describir todo del amor que tengo para los cooperadores de salud, familias, y amigos que me ayudaron con este proyecto. Mil gracias a todos de ustedes. Many mentors and friends helped make this book what it is today. First, I am extremely grateful for the guidance, time, and mentorship that Mary Jo Reiff has given me over the years. Mary Jo, thank you for always making the time to read over drafts, for giving me critical and supportive feedback, and above all else, for believing in me and telling me (at a time when I was ready to quit and didn't know where I fit in) that you felt I had something important to contribute to the field. Thanks also to Amy Devitt, Frank Farmer, Suzy D'Enbeau, and Dave Tell, who helped in various ways not only to create a former version of this project as a dissertation but also to ask critically important questions at my defense that led to a reenvisioning of it into its form today.

The seeds for this project began with a social gathering with the University of Kansas Rhetoric and Composition 2Cs group, where we read "Language Difference in Writing: Toward a Translingual Approach" by Bruce Horner, Min-Zhan Lu, Jacqueline Jones Royster, and John Trimbur, and a lot of people expressed frustration about *what exactly* a translingual approach might be, and what it really looks like. Additionally, at my dissertation defense, I was asked what any of this had to do with *rhetoric*. My hope is that this book will be a proper response to those questions and a helpful resource for others who might have similar concerns.

This project was possible because of financial support from the University of Kansas Department of English and the graduate school, and the support of my colleagues from the University of Dayton and the University of Wisconsin-Milwaukee. Thank you, Andrea, from CSR, for your constant support in the early stages of this research. Gracias, Laura Gonzales, for reading and responding to drafts of this manuscript—your input was crucial to moving this forward. Many thanks to my colleagues and friends Jennifer Nish, Kenton Rambsy, Fatima Esseili, Cheryl Naruse, Shannon Toll, Meredith Doench, and Patrick Thomas for being my writing group companions and support system at various stages of writing.

To the SWR reviewers, thank you for your sharp critiques and encouraging words that helped me develop this text. Thanks, Sue Hum, for supporting my work and encouraging me to attend the SWR panel at the Conference on College Composition and Communication Annual Convention, and for introducing me to Victor. Muchísimas gracias, Victor Villanueva, for believing in this project and helping it come to fruition. You were the best fit as an editor I could ever hope for this project, and it's been an honor to work with you. Thank you also to everyone who worked with this manuscript through production, especially Bonny Graham, Ann Prisland, and Sara P. Evangelos.

Mom, Dad, and Rebecca, thanks for always being my biggest fans and steadfast support from the beginning. Thank you, Dan, for being the best partner I could ask for in life, especially during summers when I was away doing research. Thank you for your unconditional support and belief in me.

PROLOGUE

Midwest, United States
A MOTHER, AFTER HEARING ME SPEAK TO HER CHILDREN IN SPANISH: ¿De dónde eres? (*Where are you from?*)
YO: Aquí. (*Me: Here.*)
ELLA: ¿Y tu esposo? ¿Es mexicano? (*Her: And your husband? Is he Mexican?*)
YO: No, americano. (*Me: No, American.*)
She nods and smiles, continuing to ask a moment later where I learned Spanish . . .

Mérida, México
A MAN, AFTER I HAD ASKED HIM FOR DIRECTIONS: ¿Dónde aprendiste español? (*Where did you learn Spanish?*)
YO: Yo tomé clase(s) en lo(s) Estado(s) Unido(s)[1] pero aprendí como conversar más en El Salvador y la República Dominicana. (*Me: I took classes in the United States, but I learned how to converse more in El Salvador and the Dominican Republic.*)
ÉL: Ay, sí, pensé que tu español pareció como una dominicana. (*Him: Oh, yes, I thought your Spanish sounded like a Dominican.*)

Near Santiago Rodriguez, República Dominicana
MY NIECE (from my host family), who exclaims in the middle of us playing at her house en el campo: ¡Tía, te habla bien! (*. . . in the rural town/countryside: Aunt! You speak good/well![2]*)

SPEAKING SPANISH

What does it mean to speak well? What does it mean to speak "good" Spanish or English or any other language? To identify language as "good" or "bad" is to look at it from an external perspective that is socially and culturally embedded. This perspective often promotes a hierarchical view of speech and writing habits based on perceived notions of standard language use and variance from that standard. The vignettes just presented demonstrate only a few of the moments when I became self-aware of how others perceived my languaging. Why was it that this woman figured the most reasonable explanation for my (a white woman's) ability to speak Spanish was that my husband might be from México? How many other white women in the United States had she met who either did not speak Spanish or attributed their fluency to a relationship? As I told the man in Mérida, the Spanish that I have developed over the years has been influenced by my time spent in El Salvador and the Dominican Republic (DR). I knew that I had developed certain ways of speaking that would be marked as Dominican Spanish, but this was further confirmed when I was in a different Spanish-speaking country and this man was curious about why I spoke Spanish como una dominicana. What were the dialectal features that made him comment on that? And what is it that made my sobrina exclaim that I could speak well?

At its core, this book aims to examine these questions and challenge linguistic inequalities regarding the uptake of "translanguaging" as a rhetorical act. Ricardo Otheguy, Ofelia García, and Wallis Reid "define translanguaging as the deployment of a speaker's full linguistic repertoire without regard for watchful adherence to the socially and politically defined boundaries of named (and usually national and state) languages" (283). Any rhetorical discussion of dialects, or varieties, of language brings into question how they are perceived across contexts. In addition to politically and socially defined boundaries of language, race, class, and gender are just a few of the other facets that influence how individuals perceive each other's languaging. These perceptions may interfere with an individual's ability to truly translanguage and feel free to draw from his or her full linguistic repertoire in certain contexts.

While others have responded with curiosity and enlightened surprise at my Spanish languaging, their perceptions are largely based on the contexts we were in (nonacademic) and my position of privilege as a white, North American woman who could travel to various countries. Many others do not have the luxury of being perceived as novel or intelligent for these types of languaging skills (Flores and Rosa), and many institutional contexts are not accepting of the community discourse of Spanish that I have learned so much from in my time abroad. Although I have worked in institutions of higher education since graduating from college, I rarely speak Spanish within the walls of my workplace for fear of judgment from language studies professors who remind me of those who once graded me on my ability to master "standard" Spanish. Although those classes laid an important foundation for me to build on outside of the classroom, my confidence in speaking Spanish evolved outside of an academic context. This difference in how my languaging is perceived, how certain types of languaging are privileged in our classrooms, and how some individuals are constrained in their ability to draw from their full linguistic repertoires drives me to explore the rhetorical potential of translanguaging. In the pages that follow, I begin by discussing concerns in the classroom, but only as a point of reference and departure. Understanding how I came to explore the rhetoric of translanguaging begins with how I learned about language variance in the dissonant spaces between my classroom learning and my professional development as a rhetorician and medical interpreter.

MEDICAL SPANISH

During my undergraduate studies, I took an elective medical Spanish class as part of my major curriculum. "You're not pre-med? Then, why are you in this class?" I remember my peers asking, shocked that anyone would sign up for the class without an interest in pursuing a health profession. I responded with some version of "who knows if I might volunteer or work as a medical translator someday." The class was difficult for me. Based mostly on vocabulary and a bit of translation theory, much of our work involved memorizing words and phrases, and then articulating them within an imagined medical context (through written tests, oral exams, and so on). The most difficult part about studying the content was that I did not know the meaning of many of the words in English. Some words looked almost identical, with an accent or change in spelling here or there, so I was not any closer to understanding the meaning of electrocardiograma by seeing the translation, *electrocardiogram*. I constantly needed to look up words in English or ask others to explain them to me. I was aware of varying dialects of English, but this was a whole new language that made the class feel like I was trying to absorb two words from two "named languages" (English and Spanish) that appeared almost identical to me in my nonprofessional understanding of medical conditions and procedures. I was not only negotiating two languages but also struggling with unfamiliar disciplinary discourses. Needless to say, I did not retain much of the information I learned; this was probably also due to the fact that I would not be called on to translate in a medical setting for several years. I kept my medical Spanish textbook for future reference, por si acaso (*just in case*).

ENCOUNTERING SPANISHES OUTSIDE THE CLASSROOM

A couple of years later, I traveled to the DR for the first time. I was working as a teaching assistant with a theology study abroad course, and I acted as an interpreter and general aid to help the professor with students on the trip. I had worked in this position the previous year, on my second trip to El Salvador, and I was interested in learning more about the DR, this country en el Caribe (*in the Caribbean*). I quickly realized that many students who learned Spanish as a second language in the United States had difficulty understanding the Spanish spoken in the DR. Being the curious language lover that I am, I was more intrigued and eager to learn the local dialect of Spanish than I was upset about the dissonance between what I heard there and what I had learned in my classes. This first trip to the DR would end up serving as a crash course in language variation, since much of my classroom instruction had been based on Central American and "standard" Spanish. This was the first time I learned that rubia did not just refer to a *blonde* woman, for some of the boys were tirando coquetas (*flirting/catcalling*) and called me this word. I stopped them and asked, "Pero no soy rubia . . . eso significa que tengo pelo blanco, no?" (*But I'm not rubia . . . that means that I have blonde hair, right?*) They quickly explained that no, I definitely was a rubia, and pointed to my skin to explain why. I also learned the word cabello for *hair* on one's head, and the meaning of ahorita, which did not translate as I thought it would to *right now*, but rather meant *a little later*. Then there was one of my favorites: un chin (pronounced oo-n ch-een), which meant *just a little bit of something.*

I enjoyed learning from the communities in the rural towns we visited, so I asked the professor how I might travel back in the future. He told me that there were many doctors and dentists who travel to the DR every year but do not know any Spanish, and they were always looking for interpreters. I was appalled at the thought of anyone traveling to a country to perform medical or dental procedures without speaking the same language as the patients. How could the doctor or dentist know what the patients needed? How many errors might occur because of language barriers? This was the first time that I recognized the desire to interpret as being in an advocacy role for patients—to ensure that their words and needs were understood, and that they also understood all that was being said about their health and medical care. This led to my spending the next two summers working with a nonprofit organization called El Centro para la Salud Rural (CSR) (*The Center for Rural Health*)[3] and serving as a guide and interpreter for one high school group and two teams that were assisting the center's summer health program. By alternating graduate coursework in rhetoric and composition during the academic year and this summer work abroad, I began to dive deeper into questions about language and rhetoric in an attempt to bridge what I was learning in the classroom and experiencing in the clinics abroad.

While working with these programs in the DR, I saw myself as an advocate, interpreter, and facilitator between host communities and US visitors. I knew that these programs were fraught with issues (Van Engen; Lasker), and yet it was because of those issues that I felt called to work in the liminal spaces of these transcultural interactions. I wanted to strive to communicate in a way that helped to care for all individuals involved, while ultimately challenging the visitors to empathize with their hosts and understand their way of life as not just drastically different from their own, but also as equally human and deserving of respect. I was especially aware of the potentially negative implications of miscommunication and error within the medical program. We were dealing with people's lives and health, and it was important to me that the clinics were run with as much professionalism, respect, and quality of care as one might expect under similar material circumstances (that is, without x-rays) in the United States.

In my first year with the health program, in 2011, many interesting moments surfaced around differences in language and culture. I was intrigued with how instances of translation were negotiated by visiting practitioners and Dominican volunteers on the health team. I also began to notice my own speech developing into a more localized accent and my ability to comprehend the phrasing of this dialect improving every day. I saw this as important progress if I was going to succeed at working with and interpreting for the community members of this program. There were many moments when I remembered the difficulty of my medical Spanish class, and realized how much easier learning a language seemed within a context of repetition and tangible application. I became intimately familiar with ways of talking about dental procedures and types of pain to determine the best course of action. I would ask if the pain was like a pinch or if it got worse with hot and cold foods or beverages. I'd instruct patients what to do: escupe (*spit*) or muerde (*bite*). I learned to talk about diabetes and what blood pressure medicine they were taking (thus learning what Metformin and Atenolol were). I also interpreted instructions in the pharmacy many times: toma una tableta cada cuatro horas sin comida . . . (*take one tablet every four hours without food . . .*) and helped the pharmacists field questions from patients about their prescriptions. I was developing medical knowledge, but within a very specific context with very specific forms of Spanish to discuss health and illness. But that was what made sense—to learn to communicate and understand discourses of health that the community members used in their daily lives. If we could not do this, then what were we there for?

As US participants adjusted their Spanish to "sound more Dominican" and rephrased medical terms to reflect their patients' language use, the entire team began to privilege the local dialect and community discourses of health. This was, in my opinion, the best rhetorical move the health providers could make to be intentional and ethical with their languaging and healthcare. Following my first year with the program, I developed a qualitative study to examine these rhetorical moves among languages, and to learn from local residents and visiting practitioners about how they responded to cultural and linguistic differences in their work together.

It is with deep gratitude to the health practitioners and local volunteers with whom I have worked that I present their stories as part of this book. They taught me about translanguaging before I even knew the terms "translingual" or "translanguaging" existed. Entonce(s), no(s) vamo(s) pa'lante. (*So, let's go forward.*)

1

Toward a Rhetoric of Translanguaging

IN THIS BOOK, I PRESENT A THEORETICAL FRAMEWORK for the rhetoric of translanguaging based on practices developed within a specific, multicultural healthcare context. Building on important work in the field (Smitherman and Villanueva; Prendergast; Gilyard) to interrogate what it means to have structurally embedded hierarchies of language and the ways that race, culture, and context influence how groups of people "language" together, I present translanguaging as a rhetorical act that can transform the ways that practitioners and communities communicate together. Specifically, I highlight the *rhetorical* nature of translanguaging in its aims to challenge linguistic inequality and promote more just social structures. I will also introduce the concept of "translation spaces" where translation work is required for negotiating meaning making across modes, languages, and discourses. I identify translation spaces as sites for transformation; when used rhetorically, translanguaging within medical translation spaces can promote patient needs, advocate for their language use, and "flip the script" of professional medical discourse as being the language of power. This encourages an intentional approach to privileging the language use and needs of the marginalized speaker in any situation. Although I discuss translanguaging in relation to how it can be used in medical translation, this rhetorical approach can apply to other spaces that require negotiating language variance in writing and speaking. This dynamic and rhetorical view of translation spaces can help us identify the complex translanguaging practices our students might engage in throughout their professional lives.

I hope the specific examples of translanguaging from this study will enhance understanding for multilingual studies of writing and rhetoric through a look at interactions in social settings outside of the classroom, and outside of predominantly English-speaking and US contexts. Additionally, this book serves to create a dialogue between discussions of the translingual and translanguaging in linguistics and rhetoric and composition programs. By focusing on the population of two rural towns of the Dominican Republic, my study examines translanguaging within a context where the spoken Spanish would be stigmatized by any other academic, theoretical, or outsider perspective. Working with a healthcare program situated within these specific communities allowed me to examine ways that the local community discourse became the dominant discourse of our clinics, and thus how the ways that my participants translanguaged reflected an alteration of power relations, a complication of language ideologies, and a preference for the languaging of their patients.

To explain the connections among translanguaging, rhetoric, and translation, I need to discuss these terms to draw together how I went from noticing languaging in the field to developing a theory about the rhetoric of translanguaging. Having developed this project over several years (2012–2017) when the fields of writing and rhetoric were being inundated with discussions of language diversity, variance, and the translingual, my terminology and my understanding of what I was studying were in constant revision. As new scholarship emerged, I worked to review and consider what the new terminology and explanations of multi- and translingual phenomena entailed. At times, I felt overwhelmed trying to keep up with all of the emerging understandings of these concepts, because there have been so many. I was grateful for the focus on language diversity in our fields, but I was trying to figure out how to make sense of the topic within the context of my study. I was also acutely aware of how the conversation was developing, and it was important for me not to take up every term or description that seemed relevant.

Throughout this project, I remained firmly grounded in the words and experiences of my participants. I wanted to privilege and forefront their descriptions of how they languaged even if they did not call it "languaging." Using Ofelia García and Li Wei's definition, languaging is "the simultaneous process of continuous becoming of ourselves and our language practices, as we interact and make meaning in the world" (8). Although my initial understanding of translingual and translanguaging phenomena began in writing studies, I realized that it was the *rhetoric* of translanguaging, and the work of applied and educational linguistics, that resonated with what my participants were describing and experiencing with their negotiation of linguistic and cultural differences, including the stigma and dissonance between their classroom-learned languaging and applied languaging in this context. And so, in the pages that follow, I address the major terms that have informed my vision for the rhetoric of translanguaging and its implications for communicative interactions and community building. Drawing from this vision, pedagogical moves to value and examine the diverse language resources of our students can also be advocated for, as well as moves to professionalize and prepare them to work with diverse audiences in their future careers. Situated within a healthcare context, this book also illuminates the imperative for emerging healthcare professionals to learn about rhetoric within multilingual environments and understand how they can advocate for their patients' discourses of health. Finally, my hope is that this theoretical framework for the rhetoric of translanguaging might help bridge studies of linguistic diversity across rhetoric, writing studies, second language studies, and applied linguistics.

TRANSLINGUAL LITERACY

A growing number of scholars in rhetoric and composition studies argue for a translingual approach to literacy practices in relation to teaching writing. Scholars such as Bruce Horner, Min-Zhan Lu, Jacqueline Jones Royster, John Trimbur, and Suresh Canagarajah have established the term "translingual" as more fitting than "multilingual" to describe literacies that incorporate cross-language relations in a way that reflects the fluidity and movement among dialects and languages in literacy today. Translingual literacy scholarship works to dismantle the idea that being multilingual, or having competence in multiple languages, is a quality that inhibits students from success in writing and speaking. According to Horner, Lu, Royster, and Trimbur in "Language Difference in Writing: Toward a Translingual Approach," this approach to writing "sees difference in language not as a barrier to overcome or as a problem to manage, but as a resource for producing meaning in writing, speaking, reading, and listening" (303). The US composition classroom has proven to be an important space to study this translingual approach, especially with the field's history of being associated with nationalistic English-only politics (Horner and Trimbur).

In the words of Paul Kei Matsuda, "translingual writing is all the rage among scholars and teachers of writing in the United States" (478). A well-established concept in the fields of linguistics and second language (L2) studies, terms related to the translingual have seen a sudden influx of interest over the past decade in the fields of writing and rhetoric. A steady increase in the number of research projects, pedagogical conversations, and debates over translingual writing, translingualism, and translingual practice have demonstrated a sincere interest, and at times confusion, about the role of the translingual in rhetoric and writing today. Scholars in linguistics and L2 studies have warned scholars of rhetoric and writing to be careful with their use of translingual scholarship and not to ignore the existing conversations in other disciplines on translingual writing (Atkinson et al.).

Some of the most influential work in rhetoric and writing studies comes from a scholar who has published in all of these disciplines (linguistics, L2 studies, rhetoric and composition): Suresh Canagarajah. In *Translingual Practice: Global Englishes and Cosmopolitan Relations*, Canagarajah explains that the term "monolingual" may be nothing more than something with academic and ideological significance because communities and communication have "always been heterogeneous. Those who are considered monolingual are typically proficient in multiple registers, dialects, and discourses of a given language" (8). Since communities are already engaging in multiple discourses, theory on translingual literacy should develop from detailed study of those communities' social practices. Understanding language difference as the norm thus requires that translingual scholarship focus on discursive interactions representing a variety of languages and dialects to better integrate theory and practice.

A turn to this approach emerged from a concern for students whose linguistic diversity has traditionally been identified as a deficit in relation to English rather than as a resource in literacy practices (Horner, Lu, Royster, and Trimbur). A translingual approach emphasizes difference as the norm even within languages identified as standard (Lu and Horner) or individuals identified as monolingual. However, the implementation of translingual theory in pedagogy and practice often remains challenged by constraints of academic institutions and expectations of colleagues (You taught them to write [academic English], didn't you?). The privileging of Edited American English (EAE) in US universities, and composition's historical ties to it, presents an undeniable conflict within the context of translingual moves in composition classrooms. There are also a number of writing teachers who struggle with the persistent ambiguity about what exactly translingual writing or translanguaging is and how to evaluate it. I do not refer to the many colleagues who are already part of the translingual conversation, but rather, to the many others I have met and heard from who do not know what to do with these calls for translingual approaches or do not understand how these approaches fit into how they were taught to teach composition within (predominantly) "English" departments. Additionally, students may question the practical implications for their future careers of taking this approach to writing and communicating. As my own students have argued, while "it sounds nice in theory," the utility of translanguaging outside of our classroom is complicated by academic and professional discourses that continue to privilege EAE.

By taking a step outside of our classrooms and institutional contexts, we can research and understand translingual rhetoric and writing in new ways that challenge "deficit" models and complicate hierarchies that place certain dialects over others. By examining how various social and cultural contexts privilege ways of speaking that are different from our academic institutions, our understanding of translingual practice will inherently grow. What many bi- and multilingual individuals already know (and what many scholars have reiterated time after time) is that communities are polyvocal and multilingual, and they translanguage in innovative ways. However, these innovative tactics are often difficult to understand when situated within a pedagogical context entrenched in institutional values and constraints. I do not argue that constraints and marginalization of speakers do not exist outside of schools—they clearly do—but there are certain unique conditions that can illuminate what a step away from the classroom can do for our discussions of standard language use, "deviance" from norms, and what is "appropriate" for certain settings. I say this not to preach to the translingual choir about what they already know, but to clearly break down these concepts in a way that invites scholars who do not quite understand the translingual conversation, or do not see themselves as part of it yet, to consider the rhetorical potential of translanguaging. Although many important studies have examined migrations, literacies, and movements of students and community members from other countries into the United States (Alvarez: Vieira; Lorimer Leonard), this book examines a context that developed from a move outward and into a predominantly Spanish-speaking context. This context illuminates the prevalence of stigma that surfaces from deficit-based models of language and the racism and classism present in perspectives on global Spanishes.

VARIATION OR DEVIANCE FROM THE "STANDARD"

The academic and professional spaces that our students inhabit and envision for their future do not openly value linguistic diversity as the norm, and yet they should. That is the issue that many linguists, rhetoricians, and compositionists have been trying to address: language variation is normal, and no dialect is inherently better than others based on linguistic features alone. However, the dissonance between theoretical calls to value linguistic variance and the social stigma placed on certain varieties more than others remains entrenched in daily practices and responses to speech and writing. This dissonance is connected to individual and societal understandings of "standard" and "nonstandard" forms of language use. Language use identified as standard has been lauded as that which connects people across differences by establishing shared codes for communicating. However, because of the affinity for teaching common codes and standard academic writing, many dialects and ways of speaking and writing have been marginalized, stigmatized, and literally stripped from students and their parents (Anzaldúa; National Museum of the American Indian; ICMN Staff). Writing teachers have responded to the linguistic imperialism of EAE by finding various ways to discuss and incorporate students' personal varieties of language use into the classroom and scholarly conversations, most often referring to home and community literacies (Heath; Flower; Cushman, *The Struggle and the Tools*).

Similarly, in language education, teachers have employed the term "appropriateness" to identify where and when certain varieties are to be used as part of a student's set of linguistic resources. Nelson Flores and Jonathan Rosa explain that

> additive approaches to language education affirm nonstandard varieties of English and nonstandard varieties of languages other than English as practices that are appropriate for out-of-school contexts but insist that students add standard conventions to their linguistic repertoires because these are the linguistic practices appropriate for a school setting. (153)

Further, Flores and Rosa argue that raciolinguistic ideologies "produce racialized speaking subjects who are constructed as linguistically deviant even when engaging in linguistic practices positioned as normative or innovative when produced by privileged white subjects" (150). The similarities between language education and composition pedagogy on this subject of appropriateness illuminates a conflict that instructors and students encounter when trying to discuss and respond to linguistic difference in the classroom. The

Students' Rights to Their Own Language (SRTOL) movement and other advocacy on behalf of students who may experience dissonance between home and school literacies have made important advances in how we examine the needs and language practices of an increasingly diverse student body. These concerns about the historical deficit-based models of both writing and language instruction have inspired much of the scholarship today on approaching language variation as a resource to draw from, rather than as an inhibitor to development.

The intersection and overlap among conversations about marginalized speakers—whether using various dialects of English or other languages—present a shared, yet at times conflicting, mission for language and writing education today. As we push toward more nuanced views of linguistic variance and translingual moves, we must acknowledge the racialized and stigmatized political, social, and cultural factors at play with how languages are used and perceived in our students' everyday lives. In "The Rhetoric of Translingualism," Keith Gilyard discusses how "the translanguaging subject generally comes off in the scholarly literature as a sort of linguistic everyperson, which makes it hard to see the suffering and the political imperative as clearly as in the heyday of SRTOL" (285). Also, he argues,

> Related to the issues of students' language rights and institutional standards is the tendency to flatten language differences in some theorizing about translingualism. Translingualists are clear about the fact that we all differ as language users from each other and in relation to a perceived standard. Often elided, however, is the recognition that we don't all differ from said standard in the same way. Given that context matters, a concept that is a key component of translingual analysis, one would always want to be careful not to level difference this way. (286)

Gilyard's statement is an important critique of how translingual scholarship may create dissonance between the groups of people that it works to advocate for. If we are to engage in research and teaching about language diversity, we must do it in a way that does not result in "a devaluing of the historical and unresolved struggles of groups that have been traditionally underrepresented in the academy and suffer disproportionately in relation to it" (286). We must also strive to avoid "the danger of translingualism becoming an alienating theory for some scholars of color" (284).

One of the first steps in restructuring our theory and pedagogy about linguistic diversity is to examine the varying degrees of stigma placed on various dialects, and the innate connection between racism and languaging in US society today through a lens of raciolinguistic ideologies. To clearly call out these prejudicial forces is critical in dismantling their power and undercutting the ideologies they reinforce. What this requires is an acknowledgment of difference within difference, whether it be varied dialects, accents, intonations, or terminology. As Ellen Cushman describes, "Understanding the differences within difference as the norms of all utterances can help imagine one type of epistemic delinking that invites a pluriversality of knowledges and languages" ("Translingual" 238). One way we can examine this difference within difference among intersections of language, race, culture, gender, and class is through translanguaging.

TRANSLANGUAGING

Though at times the terms translanguaging and translingual have been used synonymously in writing studies, I want to clarify that my use of these terms comes explicitly from García's work, which most often relates to educational and applied linguistics. In line with her definition of translanguaging as being transdisciplinary, I draw from these definitions and expand on them to specifically discuss their application to rhetoric within a healthcare setting. I build on her (and other applied linguists') use of translanguaging because it holds great potential for rhetorical study.

In *Translanguaging: Languaging, Bilingualism and Education*, García and Wei provide the following definition:

> Translanguaging refers to the act of languaging between systems that have been described as separate, and beyond them.

As such, translanguaging is transformative and creates change in interactive cognitive and social structures that in turn affect our continuous languaging becoming. Finally, in its transdisciplinarity, translanguaging enables us as speakers to go beyond traditional academic disciplines and conventional structures, in order to gain new understandings of human relations and generate more just social structures, capable of liberating the voices of the oppressed. (42)

Drawing from both cognitive and social structures, this approach acknowledges the connections across domains and disciplines to gain new understandings of human relations. What can be distinctly rhetorical is the potential of translanguaging to generate more just social structures in an effort to liberate the voices of the oppressed. In "Translanguaging as Process and Pedagogy: Developing the English Writing of Japanese Students in the US," García and Naomi Kano define translanguaging as a process that is used "to give voice to new sociopolitical realities by interrogating linguistic inequality" (261). This unlocks the power to create more just structures—when rhetorical approaches to translanguaging are used to interrogate linguistic inequality. By interrogating linguistic inequality, we are directly addressing Gilyard's concerns about flattening difference and making space for restructuring hierarchies of language through new understandings of the contextualized stigmatization and marginalization of certain dialects over others.

Bringing linguistic inequality into the forefront of our translanguaging conversation requires an examination of the social construction of named languages. In "Clarifying Translanguaging and Deconstructing Named Languages: A Perspective from Linguistics," Otheguy, García, and Reid "define translanguaging as the deployment of a speaker's full linguistic repertoire without regard for watchful adherence to the socially and politically defined boundaries of named (and usually national and state) languages" (283). Bi- and multilingual individuals may recognize translanguaging as something they can do in certain contexts, but they also might acknowledge that there are many times when they adhere to socially and politically defined boundaries of named languages.

Otheguy, García, and Reid argue that since named languages cannot be defined linguistically, they are not linguistic objects (286). Instead, the authors explain that when they use the term "linguistic repertoire," it refers to someone's idiolect: "a person's own unique, personal language, the person's mental grammar that emerges in interaction with other speakers and enables the person's use of language" (289), which comes from the internal perspective of an individual rather than external perspectives of society. Clarifying their purpose, the authors explain that the "ordered and categorized lexical and grammatical features" of an idiolect "are the things that linguists actually analyze and study, not a named language even when, confusedly, they use named languages to report on their research . . . [such as] French, English, and Spanish. These categories are not linguistic but socio-cultural, and as such are extraneous to the enterprise of analyzing the idiolectal features" (289). The dissonance between the discussion of the linguistic and the sociocultural is also where many writing and rhetorical scholars encounter issues with our current conversations on translanguaging. Saying that one "speaks English" or "speaks Spanish" acknowledges the importance of an outsider's perspective, reflecting social norms with how others perceive us (293), and while this may not be the focus of study for linguistics, it is the focus of rhetoric.

Outsiders' perspectives, influences, and persuasive tactics are squarely within a rhetorical analysis of languaging. Rhetoricians want to know why people language in the ways they do and how people might influence an audience, or be influenced by audiences, in their development of languaging. Although Otheguy, García, and Reid distinguish what would be best for understanding an individual's personal linguistic competence and how named language categories are separate from that, a rhetorical approach *would* be interested in the social purposes and inequality that results from named languages and their use in society.

RHETORIC AND TRANSLANGUAGE WORK

The potential for understanding translanguaging as a rhetorical concept begins with a look at how individuals use rhetorical attunement and rhetorical sensibilities to navigate complex language situations. In "Multilingual Writing as Rhetorical Attunement," Rebecca Lorimer Leonard shows "how writing across languages and locations in the world fosters what might be thought of as *rhetorical attunement*: an ear for, or a tuning toward, difference or multiplicity. Rhetorical attunement is a literate understanding that assumes multiplicity and invites the negotiation of meaning across difference" (228). This concept has great potential for fostering a vision of any speech or writing event as inherently polyvocal and full of variation. By assuming multiplicity, we are open to taking the first moves toward rhetorical attunement in a negotiation of linguistic, cultural, and embodied ways of communicating. Lorimer Leonard explains, "Rhetorical attunement highlights the rhetorical in multilingualism: its instability and contingency, its political weight and contextual embeddedness. In fact, calling attunement rhetorical serves to underline these elements—materiality, contingency, emergence, resistance" (230). These rhetorical components of multilingualism further demonstrate the importance of analyzing contextual and political factors that influence translanguaging. The rhetoric of translanguaging begins at this contextual embeddedness and critically approaches translanguaging with an awareness of material and sociocultural factors that influence communication.

Further drawing from this focus on rhetoric and context, Juan Guerra brings the notion of "rhetorical sensibility" to the forefront of conflicts that arise when we try to integrate translingual theory into the writing classroom. In "Cultivating a Rhetorical Sensibility in the Translingual Writing Classroom," Guerra argues that

> we falter in our efforts to help our students understand what a translingual approach is because we have been leading them to think that we expect them to produce a particular kind of writing that mimics what we call code-meshing rather than getting them to understand that what we want instead is for them to call on the rhetorical sensibilities many of them already possess but put aside because of what they see as a jarring shift in context. (231–32)

It is this jarring shift in context that I can relate to in my own teaching and conversations about translingual approaches to writing and rhetoric. In many teachers' efforts to integrate code-meshing (Young; Young and Martinez; Canagarajah, "Codemeshing") into the classroom, the focus too often returns to a product rather than a process of negotiating language, context, and cultural factors. This contextual difference brings up questions about whether students can, should, or would even want to code-mesh in the classroom. In describing his students' experience of being asked to translanguage in a classroom, Guerra explains,

> The school context lacked the social, personal, and inter-relational stakes—as well as the intimate, rhetorical familiarity—that they readily found at home with their friends and families. The mistake I made . . . is that I inadvertently assumed that students can ignore the circumstances they face in the new rhetorical situation (an assigned essay in a classroom) and can easily transfer their language practices from one site to another. In other words, I failed to acknowledge that I was asking students to do the same thing with language in two rhetorically different and highly situated settings. (231)

Not only does Guerra highlight the contextual embeddedness of code-meshing, but he also mentions the importance of relationships and rhetorical familiarity. This key component of relationships brings into question concepts of trust, interrelational stakes, and intimacy for language use. Language use is always personal and political, so to expect students to engage in translanguaging with their classmates and teachers in the same ways that they do with their family members and close friends is to disregard the institutional context in which the classrooms are located and the differences in power relations of the various contexts where students may translanguage.

Individuals do not translanguage in a vacuum; they have audiences, social interactions, and dialogues that help with the development of their languaging repertoires. Lorimer Leonard explains that "language—the stuff of a resource—is something we make as we move rather than something static we carry around; and resources, then, must also be externally influenced and socially practiced" (232). Languaging does not "belong" to certain domains such as school or home, but "the languaging is that of the learner, his or her own being, knowing and doing, as it emerges through social interaction" (García and Wei 80). While languaging belongs to the learner, it emerges through social interaction, and therefore, if it will be used for rhetorical purposes, a type of relationship building must happen to make it effective. Therefore, my notion of rhetoric in "the rhetoric of translanguaging" draws from Jeffrey Grabill's positioning of rhetoric as

> the art designed for the persistent burden of detecting shared problems, guiding inquiry, and shaping responses. It is empirical, pragmatic, and collective. The rhetor is not and perhaps never has been the individual, the good man speaking well. But there are specific, key roles for individuals with this art of rhetoric. Indeed, it requires lots of individuals pulling together to do the rhetoric imagined here. ("Work" 259)

This vision of rhetoric illuminates the need for collective linguistic resources. By drawing on each group member's linguistic resources, a collective approach to rhetoric can be even more powerful and effective for the varied linguistic and cultural needs of specific audiences. By coming together, individuals can translanguage in innovative ways that may provide new insights into solving problems and pursuing shared goals.

RELATIONSHIP BUILDING

When a group of individuals from different linguistic and cultural backgrounds are placed in a setting and expected to translanguage together, certain conditions must be met to allow them to explore and execute this successfully. First, they must understand *why* it is that they will translanguage together. For what purpose have they been brought together? A shared goal or unifying purpose can then help them identify *how* they will move forward in attempting to translanguage. For the participants in this study, that shared goal was to provide healthcare for the local community members. This shared purpose provided a context, and any misunderstanding presented an exigency for a specific kind of rhetorical situation (Bitzer) with languaging: they needed to translanguage, and do it convincingly, in order to be rhetorically effective in providing care and responding to patient needs. In order to accomplish this, they also needed to trust each other and be willing to take risks together in performing language in new ways. Intentionally building relationships supported all other aspects of the rhetoric of translanguaging because it helped the individuals draw from collective resources, feel solidarity in their struggles with language variation, and persevere toward new forms of communicating and problem solving.

Recognizing the various words, gestures, dialects, and other communal linguistic resources that individuals can pull from when working in a group will allow them to develop creative ways to translanguage across differences. Throughout this process of identifying a purpose and developing strategies for translation and translanguaging, relationships must be developed to establish trust, mutual understanding, and innovative approaches to languaging. However, since translanguaging challenges linguistic inequality, individuals may find themselves face-to-face with moments that highlight the injustice in how their own languaging is used and perceived by others in various contexts. Ideally, if the group is able to critically deconstruct these social factors and understandings of named languages, then its members can move beyond the hierarchical structures that limit their translanguaging potential.

Relationship building serves as a foundation for any kind of productive translanguaging, and it brings into question the potential for drawing from collective resources, rather than individual performances. A step outside the classroom and into lived contexts can further our understanding of why and how our integration of translingual theory into practice, or practice into theory, must begin with how it happens in "highly situated settings" (231), as Guerra points out. Whether our concerns lie in pedagogical approaches, professional development, or practical application, the desire to encourage collaboration and collective action is highly regarded in many institutional and communal contexts.

COMPLICATING LANGUAGE IDEOLOGIES

The rhetoric of translanguaging complicates language ideologies when individuals are faced with language variation in their interactions. The ways we perceive and respond to differences indicate our beliefs about language and specific language users. Language ideologies may surface when analyzing how individuals take up translation to remedy variance in their languaging together. If translanguaging comes from the perspective of the speaker drawing from his or her full linguistic repertoire, then translation is a response to a specific exigency of misunderstanding or clashing codes between individuals. For example, if I speak to you by drawing from my own linguistic resources, I will try to pick and choose linguistic codes that I assume (or know) to be mutually understood and used by you. However, when a disruption happens in our languaging together—you do not understand my use of a certain word, or I cannot comprehend the phrasing you use—then we turn to a type of "translation"[1] to respond to that language variation between us. This translation negotiates meaning and seeks to ensure that our listener or audience (me for you and you for me, in this case) can understand the word(s) initially uttered in a way that makes sense within their existing linguistic repertoire. Translanguaging can occur on its own without translation; however, when individuals translate to remedy dissonance in their understanding of each other, translanguaging can serve as part of that translation process as well. Translation incorporates a translanguaging approach only when individuals draw from their full linguistic repertoire and privilege marginalized speakers in situations of power differentials.

If I work as a medical interpreter, I am constantly responding to this exigency of disparate codes and attempting to bridge connections across them by transforming the words spoken in one way of languaging by the physician into a related, but different way of languaging by the patient, and vice versa. How I approach my role as interpreter depends on my ideologies about language and translation. If I hold certain biases related to language hierarchies, that will influence the ways I choose to move forward, or how I may be resistant to certain forms of communicating. The rhetoric of translanguaging complicates language ideologies to make space for open dialogue and respect among differences. Coming from an understanding of translanguaging and a concern for marginalized speakers, I may choose to specifically draw from contextual, material, and ideological factors that rhetorically position my "translations" in a way that privileges the marginalized speaker within specific contexts. Additionally, this approach may push me as an interpreter to move beyond the limitations of "standard" dictionaries and translation guidebooks. Similar to how a classroom approach to translanguaging moves outside of EAE and standardized language systems, translanguaging as an interpreter leads to moving outside of standard interpreter training tools and practices.

CULTIVATING TRANSLATION SPACES

If a group of individuals (whether students, workplace teams, or community members) have shared goals and encounter differences in their languaging about a topic, they must *cultivate space* for translation in order to find common ground and move forward in conversation. They need to decide how to foster translation spaces to help connect with each other and their potential audience(s) amid moments of difference in meaning and languaging. Earlier I defined a translation space as any space that requires some type of translation work across different forms of meaning making through modes, languages, and discourses. Within translation spaces, individuals negotiate meaning across various boundaries of writing, speaking, languages, and institutional and communal discourses. Considering translation as occurring within spaces that cultivate moves across modes, languages, and discourses can illuminate the complexity, dynamic fluidity, and multiple participants and texts that negotiate language in the rhetoric of translanguaging. Translation spaces call attention to the exigency of misunderstanding between individuals by setting forth some type of translation or interpretation that is necessary to develop mutual understanding. This may look very different depending on the context and individuals, but its foundation for continuous languaging and collaboration remains consistent.

At times, two individuals may call in a third group member to help facilitate the conversation because she or he has more overlap in linguistic repertoire and cultural knowledge with both parties. Whatever way this translation space is cultivated, it is only sustained if there has been, and continues to be, a type of relationship building among the individuals involved. These connections will build trust, promote the development of shared languaging, and help individuals feel more comfortable negotiating language variation. Without relationships and rhetorical familiarity, speakers will give up on the interaction, or resist engaging with others whom they perceive to have little overlap with their own linguistic repertoires.

CRITICALLY REINVENTING DISCOURSE

Various cultural, religious, and institutional values may influence how collectives approach translation spaces. The potential for critical reinvention comes with an intention to challenge discourses of power and reinvent discursive tactics in ways that reflect community values and terminology, rather than an assumption that the discourse of power is always the "best" languaging to use. Not all of my participants accomplished this critical reinvention in their time together. However, through a few examples of how the local community members influenced our translanguaging and translation spaces, I will demonstrate how this critical reinvention is possible. With an intentional move toward rhetorical translanguaging, critical reinvention can be positioned as a goal for long-term interactions among individuals from various institutions and communities.

Figure 1 shows the interaction among these key components of the rhetoric of translanguaging. This diagram is intentionally interactive and continuous because all of these factors play into each other in various ways. To understand the intentionality of the rhetoric of translanguaging, relationship building must begin the process of individuals choosing to translanguage together. When they encounter language variation in their communication with others, they may be faced with language ideologies that encourage or hinder their interactions together. By complicating those language ideologies that perceive certain languaging as being better or worse, the collective can be reflexive in its biases and pursue language use that reflects its context and goals as a group. As individuals cultivate translation spaces, they may encounter variances across written, spoken, dialectal, and discursive languaging about shared topics of conversation. By cultivating translation spaces across these modes, languages, and discourses, they can negotiate meaning and encourage a collaborative approach to developing mutual understanding. From those translation spaces, critical reinvention of discourse may be taken up between institutions and communities. Individuals and the collective will negotiate cultural differences and develop new ways to communicate that privilege community discourses over institutional discourses or move back and forth among the various discourses. Then, ideally, they will continue to build relationships from those encounters with language variation, and will evolve in their translanguaging to continue the process of growing in their work and languaging together.

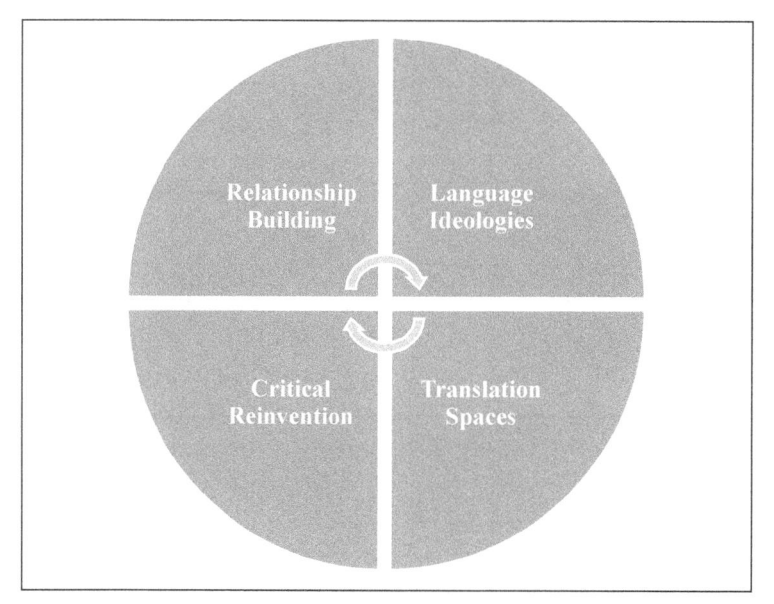

Figure 1. The rhetoric of translanguaging.

Certain spaces place translation and translators at the epicenter of interaction. The patient-interpreter-provider triad within a clinical setting is the specific translation space I examine in this text, but translation spaces and moments happen in any number of other professional, institutional, and communal settings where individuals come together for a common goal or shared purpose. Figure 2 is a Venn diagram illustrating how this translation space works in healthcare. Simply integrating a third party into communicative interactions forces us to examine translanguaging in new ways that account for the dynamic interactions that can happen when people negotiate languages through translation together. As shown in Figure 2, each section that is not shared with any other part represents the individual's linguistic repertoire. When the individuals encounter each other in a clinical space, the middle section shared by all parties represents the dynamic space of translanguaging that brings them all together. The shared sections between the interpreter and the patient and the interpreter and the healthcare provider represent overlap in their shared languaging abilities. The interpreter has certain ways of talking about and understanding concepts that are shared with the provider and with the patient. She or he may negotiate terminology in those spaces to pursue mutual understanding with either party. Finally, the shared space between the provider and the patient represents any shared languaging between them and the embodied communication in the exchange. Although embodied forms of language occur throughout the entire translation space (especially for sign language interpreters), they are especially pronounced between the provider and patient. This may take the form of a provider reading the patient's expressions or examining his or her body; it may also represent how the patient reads the provider's posture and embodied responses to the conversation and exam.

The interpreter translanguages in ways that negotiate various material, linguistic, and rhetorical factors to bridge understanding between the patient and the healthcare provider. The interpreter's approach to *how* the conversation is pushed forward identifies a rhetorical purpose: to support the expressions, needs, and perfor-

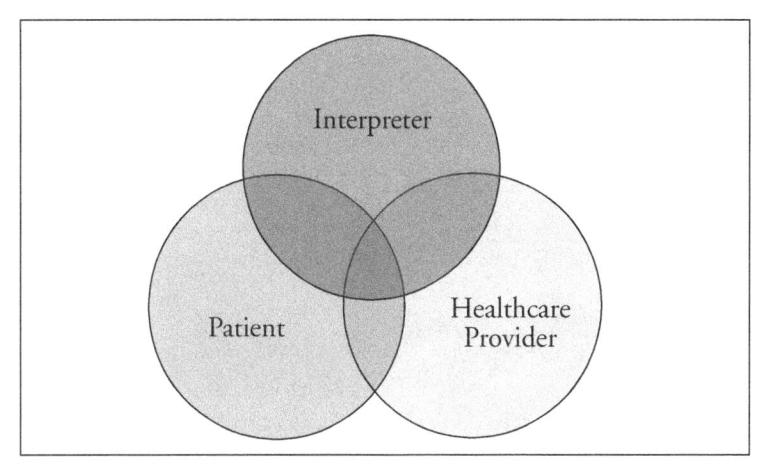

Figure 2. Medical translation space.

mance of either or both the patient and the provider. By cultivating an interactive dialogue that draws from all available means and modes of communicating, the interpreter can also incorporate translanguaging in a rhetorical way that privileges the discourse of the patient.

Drawing on this understanding of translation spaces as sites of linguistic and cultural negotiation, in Chapters 3 and 4, I examine how translation spaces were cultivated to privilege the community discourse over "professional" ways of speaking about health and illness. By viewing the Spanish of the US professionals as a Spanish in need of translation, versus the patient having a deficit in communication abilities, some of our translation spaces demonstrated the rhetoric of translanguaging. One of the goals of this rhetorical approach to translanguaging is to explore how it might help our students develop into more caring and culturally aware professionals, and how it can do the difficult work of exposing inequality and fighting for a more holistic view of people's varied language practices. But before moving onto a deeper examination of these concepts, in Chapter 2 I describe my research design and the context for this study.

2

Research Design

I BEGAN TO DESIGN THIS STUDY BY CONSIDERING questions I had about how communication across difference works, and what practical strategies multilingual rhetors use to achieve mutual understanding. I wanted to know why language and information transfer happened in certain ways during CSR's summer healthcare program, or why things went wrong, and how what I might learn could contribute to existing theories on border crossings of language, culture, and nation. In addition to the individual processes of navigating language variation, I was curious about the collective uses of translanguaging. How do groups of people negotiate languages to navigate rhetorical moves across differences in workplace settings? What might an investigation into the communicative practices of a specific team working with cross-cultural healthcare demonstrate for rhetorical theories of languaging?

These points of inquiry reflect how Bruce Horner, Samantha NeCamp, and Christiane Donahue hope a move toward the translingual "shifts our focus away from individuals, located on a fixed scale of competence toward 'mastery' of a reified 'target' language, and toward groups of people working in collaboration to use all available linguistic resources" (288). Transitioning from the focus on individual rhetors to collective action is helpful for exploring the rhetoric of translanguaging within this situated healthcare context. This perspective allows for an investigation into all of the interpreters, literacy sponsors (Brandt), and team-building efforts that enable the integration of translanguaging in professional spaces. Thus, this project was designed with the following research questions in mind: (1) What strategies do transnational healthcare program participants and local volunteers develop to negotiate meaning and mutual understanding with varied levels of proficiency in different languages? (2) How can the study of communication within these specific transnational healthcare clinics inform understanding of collaboration across cultural and linguistic differences?

CONTEXT OF STUDY[1]

Each summer, El Centro para la Salud Rural (CSR) works with a Catholic, midwestern university to host a five-week trip for US-based healthcare students and professionals to the Dominican Republic. The summer program's purpose is to provide accessible medical and dental services to rural communities while fostering cross-cultural relationships with local volunteers who help run the clinics and host the visiting participants. Based in Santiago de los Caballeros, CSR administrators choose 6 (from more than 150 affiliated) communities each year to host summer program clinics. Communities that have the opportunity to host clinics often do so for a maximum of two to three years in a row. These clinics provide general medical and dental care for individuals who experience limited access to healthcare services because of geographic and socioeconomic factors. Increasingly, the summer program has also incorporated local Dominican physicians from the region to travel with groups and work in the clinics. Throughout the remainder of the year, CSR receives various local and foreign healthcare practitioners who follow up on the referrals made by the summer program doctors and the cooperadores de salud (*health promoters*). The cooperadores are leaders in the affiliated communities, and are chosen and trained by the organization to serve as point people with whom local residents can share health-related concerns. During the summers of 2011 and 2012, I worked as a coordinator for the summer program with two groups and host communities in the same region. As a coordinator, I worked with an assistant coordinator to plan homestays and activities, serve as an interpreter inside and outside of the clinic, and act as the primary liaison between the host community and visiting participants.

A typical summer healthcare team usually includes one or two physicians, dentists, pharmacists, and nurses, all traveling from the United States. These professionals may vary in their nationality and residence. In the two groups I worked with, we had physicians originally from Venezuela and Nepal who were working in the United Sates, and a Dominican physician from Santiago. Additionally, one or two undergraduate US ayudantes (*helpers*) worked with the patient intake process by taking vital signs (blood pressure, pulse rate, and so on) and filling out the patient health history form. The ayudantes also provided general assistance as needed in various areas of the clinic. In addition, three to five young adults from the local community took up the ayudante's role, mostly helping with communication or letting patients know when it was their turn for a consultation. The cooperadores organized an equipo de trabajo (*work team*) of local volunteers who helped with interpretation for the intake process as ayudantes, kept track of the patient list and money, and performed various other tasks to keep the clinic running. The makeup of a local team depends on the community and individuals available to work morning clinic hours for four weeks during the summer. CSR healthcare clinics serve multiple communities in each region, so some of the Dominican volunteers I worked with in 2012 were visitors to the other clinic I had worked with in 2011, and vice versa. All participants of these multicultural healthcare teams were volunteers, and the visiting healthcare providers fundraised to pay for participating in the program.

DATA COLLECTION

I completed the data collection for this project using ethnographic methods of participant observation and interviews.[2] Additionally, I analyzed supporting documents and presentations from the orientation week for US participants to triangulate and compare findings with the experiences described in the interviews. Although I had worked with a group in 2011, the study I describe here began in 2012. Data about the group from 2011 came from interviews with participants and recall from my own journaling and memory. During June and July 2012, I participated in the summer program as a coordinator for the second time and took observational field notes. At the request of the program director, I took all of my field notes outside of clinic hours to maintain focus on my work as a coordinator for the group. If there were ever moments of downtime, I would jot notes about experiences to remember to elaborate on later.

Thomas Lindlof and Bryan Taylor explain that "participant observation is, at its core, *a role that is negotiated and performed*" (144), where the researcher may take on roles that are already available or a new role that has been created for him or her to occupy. I negotiated my roles as coordinator, interpreter, researcher, and friend on a daily basis. I was constantly aware of what Lindlof and Taylor describe as the embodied experience of this type of research. There were moments when cultural values and assumptions surfaced and collided with how others perceived me in positive and negative ways as an americana de Nueva Yor(k) (*American woman from New York*).[3] From hearing conversations about me by people who thought I did not know Spanish to making strong bonds with patients and volunteers, my understanding of how to continuously negotiate my role as a participant and observer grew with each week. Also, although my previous experience with the program established some rapport with the healthcare practitioners, it was through our interactions inside and outside of the clinic that I gradually gained their trust as someone who could provide support through medical interpretation and cultural orientation.

During June 2014, I visited CSR to attend and help out at the program's orientation. I was invited to give a presentation for the coordinators, and I attended three sessions of the beginner-level Spanish classes to learn more about the in-country preparation the program provides for participants with limited proficiency in Spanish. Part of my analysis was informed by the notes I took while attending orientation sessions and having conversations with the program director and cooperadores that week. I also analyzed three documents: the medical health history form, the participant guidebook, and a Spanish language packet for participants. Attending the Spanish classes and rhetorically analyzing these documents helped inform my understanding of how the US participants prepared for communicating in the program and what written materials were provided to aid their languaging in the campo.

INTERVIEWS

I completed twenty-three semistructured interviews with participants: ten from the Dominican Republic and thirteen from the United States. All interviewees served on the healthcare teams that I worked with in 2011 and 2012, and had Spanish or English as their primary language. Interviews with individuals from the United States were conducted in English and interviews with individuals from the Dominican Republic were conducted in Spanish. All US-based interviewees were pursuing professional or pre-professional degrees in healthcare (medicine, dentistry, nursing, and pharmacy) at the time of their participation in the program. Dominican interviewees included adult volunteers who helped with daily clinic activities and all three of the community healthcare leaders in Buena Vista and Rancho de la Vaca during those years.[4] Table 1 provides information about the participants I interviewed.

Table 1. Program Participants Interviewed

#	Country of Origin	Role in Program	Buena Vista (2011)	Rancho de la Vaca (2012)
3	DR	Cooperador/a de Salud	1	2
7	DR	Ayudante	7	0
2	US	Medical Student	1	1
2	US	Dental Student	0	2
2	US	Nursing Student	0	2
3	US	Ayudante	1	2
2	US	Pharmacy Student	0	2
2	US	Assistant Coordinator	1	1

Spanish was the primary language of all the Dominican interviewees, and English was the primary language of all the US interviewees. In their interviews, participants shared a range of named languages to describe their linguistic abilities; Table 2 provides information about these descriptions. When asked "What languages do you know how to speak and understand?" participants responded with the answers shown in this table. The first five categories, which include all twenty-three interview participants, mention English or Spanish or both; the latter five categories, which represent a subset of those interviewed, include stated language abilities in addition to Spanish or English.

I conducted interviews in person in the Dominican Republic, and in person and over the phone in the United States. When designing interviews, I aimed to develop open-ended questions that would allow the participant to describe experiences of language dif-

Table 2. Interview Participant Responses to the Question "What Languages Do You Know How to Speak and Understand?"

Spanish only	4*
Fluent in Spanish with a little English	6
Fluent in English with a little Spanish	6
Fluent in English with moderate proficiency in Spanish	3
Fluent in English with advanced proficiency in Spanish	4
Fluent in Cantonese	1
Knows a little Italian	2
Knows a little French	2
Can count in Japanese	1
Knows basic Arabic	1

*I observed at least two of these participants using English words or phrases during the program and in their interview, but they reported that they knew only Spanish.

ference and cross-cultural interactions. Questions focused on topics concerning moments of misunderstanding, working with others who were from a different nation, nonverbal communication, and instances of interpretation, among others. Holding semistructured interviews allowed for revision and rephrasing as I gradually realized what questions were not as clear as others, or which ones needed explicit follow-up questions. For additional details of my interview protocol, see the appendix.

TRANSCRIPTION AND CODING

I transcribed all interviews with a sincere attempt to represent my interviewees' natural language use as much as possible. A common trait of rural Dominican Spanish is the dropping of the letter *s* at the ends of words. So, for instance, in text quotations from Spanish transcripts, there may be a word written as nosotro(s) to represent that the full word being said was nosotros, but that it was pronounced nosotro when the interviewee stated it. After transcribing the interviews, I used comparative analysis (Corbin and Strauss) and pattern coding (Miles and Huberman) to develop thematic categories centered on moments of misunderstanding, language "barriers," translation, and other communicative strategies in the clinic. I also incorporated memoing (Miles and Huberman) and coding by hand while reviewing transcripts to note any emerging themes or connections with my field notes. Then, I turned to NVivo 10 software to aid my coding and categorizing processes.

ANALYSIS

In my initial coding and analysis, I focused a lot on the barriers that my interviewees experienced and the strategies they developed to respond to linguistic and cultural differences. Using grounded practical theory (Craig and Tracy), I analyzed the data through problem, technical, and philosophical levels to determine how interviewees used rhetorical strategies to overcome communicative problems, and to identify what situated ideals influenced how they decided whether to engage in language negotiation (Bloom).

However, when I revisited the data, my follow-up analysis focused more on how translanguaging was being used and what was rhetorical about the ways that individuals worked together to negotiate languages. I also wanted to examine how individuals were rhetorically negotiating different Spanishes, and what an examination of stigma and language ideology might do to highlight the unique execution of translanguaging in this program. Therefore, I began to reexamine the data with a focus on general categories that I felt illuminated aspects of translanguaging and rhetoric, such as language ideologies, translation, linguistic hierarchies, race, culture, and collaboration. Additionally, I reexamined data about relationship building because I felt this was a component of the study that was important to highlight in demonstrating how individuals can draw from collective resources of a group while working toward shared goals.

Because I was familiar with the data, I was able to identify key moments that I might have described as "problems" or "technical strategies" before, but that could be used to discuss more explicitly the things that became complicated (translation, language ideologies, and so on) when taking a rhetorical approach to translanguaging. This meant that I first needed to identify relevant quotations by revisiting transcripts to discover any additional or related comments that would be useful, and then analyze what the interviewees' experiences meant for my new exploration of these concepts. The most interesting development of this second round of analysis was what I found in my field notes, but had not analyzed fully before, about how language ideologies were complicated and how raciolinguistic ideologies (Flores and Rosa) were present or challenged in this temporary health program. By incorporating some of these notes and connecting them with interview data, my updated analysis allowed me to go deeper than I had before into the languaging practices and social stigma surrounding them, in an attempt to describe what my healthcare team used as strategies in response to problems.

LATER CONSIDERATIONS

While preparing for the data collection, I encountered various challenges that come with multi-institutional and multinational ethnographic projects. However, these challenges come from the added rigor of attempting to engage in cross-cultural, reciprocal, international research. First, I encountered resistance from the US institution that I was working for in conducting the research while also working in my role as coordinator. A program administrator was concerned about my priorities for the research versus my daily responsibilities as a coordinator and interpreter in the program. The US program director suggested that I take field notes outside of clinic hours, and that I seek approval from the director of CSR in Santiago as well. I received that approval and later engaged in multiple productive conversations with the US director concerning feedback from my participants about the program. Also, I initially set up this study to interview all members of the clinical healthcare team, but I did not design it to include minors. When I arrived in Rancho de la Vaca in 2012, I realized that three of our Dominican ayudantes were sixteen or seventeen years old, so any accounts of their work with the team came from other team members' interviews or from field notes that I took about conversations with them. These ayudantes were integral to our team in 2012, but they also seemed to have experiences similar to the those of young adult ayudantes I interviewed from Buena Vista; as a result, their general strategies and experiences were represented in the study despite the limitation that I did not interview them.

Other challenges with this study included the absence of interview data with patients, and insufficient time and material resources to reach all of the adult volunteers from both countries for interviews. Many patients were in town only for the day they visited the clinic, and I did not want to disrupt their time at the clinic with my research agenda. The director had asked that I not collect data during clinic hours, and follow-up outside of the clinic and program was easiest with the participants I had developed relationships with: the healthcare team volunteers. Taking field notes outside of clinic hours was another limitation on my recall of events; however, I argue that any form of field notes taken while being an active participant in a program would be somewhat delayed in order to fully participate in communicative interactions as they happen naturally in any setting.

In the following chapters, I discuss the context of my study as something that illuminates how, in the rhetoric of translanguaging, stigmatization of language is dynamic and in flux because of contextual and material factors. Whereas one way of speaking may be considered "bad Spanish" in certain institutional contexts, it can be privileged as the "best Spanish" if we think beyond that context and consider community discourses as integral to health practitioners' languaging development. In Chapter 3, I turn to the concept of "stigma" to examine how linguistic ideologies inform how languaging is perceived and taught, and then explore how the rhetoric of translanguaging can work to dismantle and move beyond those limitations. To understand these concepts, I examine the "differences within difference" (Cushman, "Translingual" 238) that my participants encountered and negotiated with Spanishes en la República Dominicana (*in the Dominican Republic*).

3

Complicating Language Ideologies

IF TRANSLANGUAGING IS A PROCESS THAT CAN "give voice to new sociopolitical realities by interrogating linguistic inequality" (García and Kano 261), then the rhetoric of translanguaging complicates language ideologies and challenges hierarchical structures of language use. The distinctly rhetorical aspect of translanguaging interrogates linguistic inequality by deconstructing how certain speakers are perceived as speaking "good" or "bad" language based on social and cultural factors of power and prestige. In this chapter, I demonstrate how language ideologies were complicated within the context of a transcultural healthcare space of the CSR program. Situated in a rural, Cibao region of the Dominican Republic, this context reveals the multiple layers of stigma and prejudice that can influence perceptions of Spanish dialects from global and local contexts. However, the dialect of Spanish that was privileged in this space *was* the regional rural dialect of Dominican Spanish. The privileging of this regional dialect was for rhetorical and professional purposes. If the healthcare providers wanted to make our clinic function, then what they learned as "professional" Spanish needed to be set aside to ensure that patients' narratives of health and illness were understood, and ultimately, that patients left the clinic with a clear understanding of how to use medications dispensed and medical advice given. This chapter examines how these participants described the Spanishes used in their time together and how those descriptions reflect a complexity of balancing stigma, theoretical prestige, and utility for effective language use in their interactions.

EL ESPAÑOL DE NOSOTROS VERSUS
EL ESPAÑOL DE USTEDES

Spanish took many forms in CSR's program, and the participants in this study recognized a few different varieties of Spanish emerging in their daily discourse. US participants mentioned five categories to describe the types of Spanish they used or encountered: *professional, American, Dominican, campo,* and *medical.* The US participants who identified the varied forms of Spanish often had an intermediate to advanced language proficiency and could recognize variances more easily. They also described this experience with language abroad as something that helped them notice distinct differences between what they had learned in school and what they encountered during their time in the Dominican Republic (DR).

Dominican participants often used a binary to describe the types of Spanish used or encountered: *Dominican* or *American* Spanish, or possessive pronouns such as *our* and *your* Spanish. When speaking to me in interviews, a few participants would clarify it as el español de nosotros or el español de ustedes (*our Spanish* or *your [plural] Spanish*). The majority of the Dominican participants would acknowledge that some US participants could "speak Spanish well" while others did not know very much. Although I identified specific categories to reflect the varieties of Spanish that my participants discussed, sometimes participants talked about "Spanish" in a general sense, without noting what type of Spanish it was. In these instances, a level of proficiency in that generalized notion of Spanish was often related to whether or not an interpreter was needed to communicate with others.

Before working with the local community for four weeks, the healthcare practitioners spent one week in Santiago for orientation. CSR's director organized this orientation week by dividing time among programming for Spanish classes, the packaging of medical supplies, cultural and historical lessons, and trips to visit museums or outreach programs in Santiago. Each morning, three different levels of Spanish classes were held for participants to familiarize themselves with conversational and medical Spanish, along with "Dominicanisms" (see Figure 3) that are commonly used in Dominican Spanish. For US participants, daily encounters with the Dominican Spanish dialect[1] revealed a number of words and phrases that had meanings different from what they had learned in their Spanish classes. Instead of calling *beans* frijoles, they were habichuelas;[2] a *public bus* was a guagua;[3] a *little bit of something* was un chin, and more. These classes were held in addition to a six-week Spanish course, which CSR's US office offered to participants prior to the program. Although the classes and texts about Dominicanisms were helpful, visitors would encounter various forms of those phrases depending on the region that they visited and the context in which they had conversations with local residents. Some communities were in the northern mountainous regions, while others, like the ones in this study, were closer to urban areas and the western side of the island. It was difficult to educate visitors on all of the possible phrases and dialectal features of Dominican Spanish before their time en el campo. What became more useful was learning within situated contexts, such as working in the clinic or helping cook a dinner, when the visitor could learn terminology and phrases in meaningful contexts that he or she would remember and likely encounter again.

For example, in Figure 3, a word such as apagón (*power blackout*) became easier to retain with our daily encounters of hearing "se fué la luz" (*the light(s) went out*) whenever the power company shut off the electricity. Alternatively, a tíguere, defined here as a *street-wise person*, was often used to describe a man who "got all the ladies" or was constantly calling on women. As my host mother taught me, one could also use the feminine version of this term to describe someone as talented or with street smarts, as in una tíguera en la cocina! (*a tiguera in the kitchen!*). The healthcare providers had various lists of Spanish vocabulary that were intended to prepare them for this trip. What they realized, though, was that the words on many of these lists did not always transfer easily into conversations. Likely as a result of recognizing how language use is not static, visitors began expanding their linguistic repertoires beyond what they may have learned in textbooks or vocabulary lists to include local

DOMINICAN LINGO

1- APAGÓN: Power blackout.
2- APLATANAO: A foreigner who has lived in the DR long enough to know what it's all about.
3- BANDERA DOMINICANA (*Dominican Flag*): Rice, beans, and meat.
4- BUQUÍ: Someone who eats a lot.
5- CANILLAS: Skinny legs.
6- CHELE: Penny.
7- CHICHÍ: Baby.
8- COLMADO: Food shop.
9- CONCHO: Public transportation car.
10- CONCON: Overcooked rice at the bottom of the pail.
11- DÍMELO!: What's up?
12- GUAGUA: Public bus.
13- GUAPO: Angry, mad.
14- JABLADOR: Liar.
15- JEVITO: Yuppie.
16- JUMO: When you've drunk too much.
17- MAMASOTA: Pretty woman.
18- MANGÚ: Plantain puree.
19- MOTOCONCHO: Motorcycle taxi.
20- PANA: Pal.
21- PAPAÚPA: Important person.
22- PARIGUAYO: "Partywatcher"; a nerd.
23- PICA-POLLO: Fried chicken.
24- PIN-PUN: The same, alike.
25- PRIETO: Black.
26- QUEDAO: Out of fashion, square.
27- TÍGUERE: A street-wise person.
28- TUMBA POLVO: Cheap flatterer.
29- UN MONTÓN: A large amount.

Figure 3. List of twenty-nine Dominicanisms from CSR's participant guidebook.

Spanish phrases that they learned while living and working with our host community. The US and Dominican volunteers experienced moments of languaging fluidly and also encountered disruptions, or what they referred to as "language barriers," when they could not understand each other. During their postprogram interviews, the participants gave names to the types of Spanish they encountered, but on a daily basis, they languaged in ways that moved among and beyond the varieties of Spanish without distinctly naming when different forms of Spanish were being used. They responded to the differences they encountered and adjusted their language use, but the actual naming did not surface in their daily interactions. In this way, they were translanguaging "without regard for watchful adherence to the socially and politically defined boundaries of named . . . languages" (Otheguy, García, and Reid 283). During the program, individuals would translanguage without constantly worrying about the socially or politically defined boundaries of Dominican or American Spanish.

Additionally, Dominicans translanguaged in ways that disregarded the named languages of English and Spanish. This surfaced in how they discussed pelota (*baseball*)—with the baseball *field* being called el play, and positions representing an accented version of el pitcher, catcher, shortstop, and so on. When describing the lexical features of Dominican Spanish, Barbara Bullock and Almeida Jacqueline Toribio explain that "the dialect is replete with borrowings from English: closet 'closet', poloché 'a polo shirt', yompa 'jumper,' è/uro' bureau, dresser', and jonrón 'home run', to name only a few" ("Reconsidering" 53). Local residents and visitors were constantly translanguaging in ways that drew from their full linguistic repertoires, or idiolects, without regard for rules separating different named languages. However, they did not always find success in understanding each other while translanguaging, and thus they turned to various forms of translation to respond to differences in their language use and develop mutual understanding. When individuals try to translanguage with others who do not have much overlap with their own linguistic repertoire, translation acts as a way to remedy dissonance in how they find common ground in the forms of communication that they do share.

In an interview with François Grosjean, García explains, "The naming of a language is always a social, political, and economic decision, not a linguistic one . . . languages are social constructs that have had very important real and material consequences in the lives of people, some bad, and some good" (Grosjean, "What Is Translanguaging?"). This point is crucial in understanding the role that rhetoric plays in studying translanguaging: if named languages are social, political, and economic constructs, it is our responsibility, as rhetoricians, to analyze and interrogate how named languages, and the social factors that construct them, influence the use and uptake of languaging in various rhetorical contexts. Studying how named languages function and reinforce hierarchies of language is rhetorical, and thus the rhetoric of translanguaging aims to challenge these hierarchies and the oppressive work they do to keep marginalized speakers in rhetorically, socially constructed "boxes" within certain spaces of power and prestige.

These spaces of power may be university classrooms, medical clinics, or any other institutional spaces that rely on disparate power relations to rationalize their existence and purpose in society. A healthcare institution has the money, resources, and individuals with knowledge who work to help patients find treatments for their ailments. A university has the money, status, and individuals with knowledge who help students advance their education and pursue careers that require a degree from a university. Named languages further complicate the power relations of these institutions because there are always certain dialects of English or Spanish or French (or others) that are privileged over other dialects, most often those associated with marginalized communities. These disempowered dialects are often disregarded or negotiated in ways that further mark individuals as "less than," while some people turn to words like "bad," "improper," or "uneducated" to describe others' language use. When individuals or communities qualify disempowered dialects in these ways, they are also qualifying the people who identify or use these dialects as bad, improper, or uneducated. If a theory of translanguaging intends to challenge these linguistic hierarchies and the social actions or policies that stigmatize language use, it must employ rhetorical moves that complicate language ideologies. To examine how individuals responded to linguistic and cultural differences in my research, I asked the US healthcare providers and Dominican volunteers how they perceived differences in Spanish and how they responded to moments when they felt they, or someone else, did not understand what was being said. What this revealed was an acknowledgment of the stigma placed on the rural Dominican dialect from a US, or global, perspective. In addition, US participants who used their version of Spanish did not always appear to be proficient Spanish speakers to the patients who visited the clinic. Dominican interviewees did not discuss the varieties of Spanish with as much complexity as did the US participants, and many of them saw the visitors as either "knowing Spanish well" or not. When Dominican interviewees wanted to converse with a US participant who did not know Spanish well, they would find me or another bilingual participant to help interpret their conversation. Similarly, US participants with limited or no proficiency in Spanish regarded Dominican Spanish as simply *Spanish*, and thus any help from Dominican ayudantes to rephrase their words *improved* their Spanish. The help of the ayudantes did improve US participants' Spanish and their interactions with the community, and many US participants began to adjust their languaging to better reflect a Dominican way of speaking. Therefore, the rural Dominican dialect of Spanish became the privileged form of language use within the context of this program.

LINGUISTIC HIERARCHIES

Local and global Spanish-speaking communities often label the rural Dominican dialect as one of the "worst" dialects of Spanish. These stigmatized views of the rural Dominican use of Spanish reflect language ideologies about correctness and class differences. Bonnie Urciuoli explains, "Ideologies of standardization and correctness particularly represent the maintenance of institutional authority. . . . Spanish correctness norms index a particularly European sense of linguistic and literary propriety (which especially contrasts with Caribbean Spanish forms and practices)" (258). With this European and Caribbean dichotomy, the underpinnings of racial and cultural differences are intertwined with how people talk about language. In "Language Variation and the Linguistic Enactment of Identity among Dominicans," Toribio examines the vernacular use of Dominican Spanish in different contexts by interviewing Dominicans who live in New York and in the region where the towns of this study are located. She argues that "the Spanish dialect of the Dominican Republic distinguishes itself in significant respects from the prescribed norm for the Spanish language. These speech forms are readily identified and recognized as being of low prestige . . . and yet, the vernacular enjoys a considerable measure of covert prestige" (1139). In Toribio's research, the region where my study took place is considered an area with a regional dialect that is "discounted or disparaged for incorporating other, less agreeable characteristics, namely those of neighboring Haiti" (1140). From both a global and a regional perspective, the Spanish that participants in this study encountered is stigmatized and undervalued. However, Toribio argues, "In this predilection for the northern Iberian variety and emphatic repudiation of the influence of the Haitian Creole, Dominicans ignore a central axiom of linguistics—language variation is normal" (1142). Although it may be normal, the stigmatization that comes with how many people respond to language variation has a real impact on social interactions and subsequent languaging. The ways that individuals respond to variation are often influenced by their ideologies and educational background regarding standard language use. Therefore, the rhetoric of translanguaging seeks to complicate these ideologies in an effort to challenge linguistic inequality.

While spending time with the host community, individuals from the United States began to notice variance between the Spanishes they had learned in class and encountered in the campo. To explain characteristics of Dominican Spanish, Lisa, a nursing student, notes that with "the grammar, they cut off . . . a lot, and they say 'ta' like ¿Cómo tú ta? instead of saying ¿Cómo estás? [*How are you?*] . . . and then for slang terms, there's the types of food like 'con con' [*overcooked rice at the bottom of the pail*],[4] or 'pin-pun' which means you look *the exact same.*" These descriptions of Dominican Spanish were related to Lisa's perceptions of "standard" and "correct" language use, most likely based on what she had learned in school. Most US participants who had an intermediate to advanced level of proficiency discussed their recognition and, at times, integration of unique characteristics of the dialect—cutting off the letter *s* at the ends of words, "slurring" words together, and using "improper" grammar. In "The Status of s in Dominican Spanish," Bullock, Toribio, and Mark Amengual explain that in sociolinguistics, "the Spanish spoken in the Dominican Republic is often described as innovative relative to other national varieties" (21), and they argue that characteristics such as *s*-deletion represent social norms associated with "Dominicanness" (23). This identification with Dominicanness resonates with how US participants told me that they would adjust their Spanish to "sound more Dominican."

Despite the integration of Dominican dialectal features into their Spanish languaging, US participants used words such as "slang," "slurring," and "improper" to describe these features, reflecting the low prestige value placed on Dominican Spanish globally. Lisa explains how even after the program, she noticed that she'd brought "that [accent] back to the United States . . . [and] every Spanish [-speaking] friend I talk to is like, 'Oh, the Dominican accent is just so ugly . . . they have one of the worst.'" This experience reveals the global hierarchy of Spanish for Lisa's friends who lived in the United States but were originally from other Latin American countries. It also demonstrates how Lisa returned home influenced by the dialect she was immersed in while abroad. She used that dialect when speaking Spanish once she returned home, but the negative reactions of her friends may have persuaded her to distance herself from speech patterns that might mark her as "sounding like a Dominican."

The words used to describe the Dominican dialect of Spanish by both the US visitors and their Spanish-speaking friends reveal an offensive hierarchical structure of Spanishes around the world. Literally calling it an "ugly" accent and one of "the worst" personifies the language use and reveals its connection with race, racism, and social status. The accent or dialect of these speakers may only be seen as "worse" in comparison to another dialect that is considered a "standard" or "pure" form of the language. Otheguy, García, and Reid explain,

> Language education has focused on teaching a version of a named language known as the standard. Such standards do not embrace all the features conventionally associated with the named language. Rather, they make room only for those features that index social prestige, that is, only those idiolectal features found in the speech of those who share a superior class membership, political power, and, in many cases, an ethnic identity. (301)

This connection between ethnic identity and language use is important to consider when examining hierarchies of Spanish, or of any named language. Not only is the rural Dominican dialect of Spanish stigmatized for US Spanish language learners and other Spanish speakers around the world, but also this specific region of the Dominican Republic is further stigmatized among Dominicans as well. Examining the intersections of language, race, and socioeconomic status reveals the complicated linguistic hierarchy that is in effect with any context of translanguaging, but especially within this context of Dominican Spanish.

LANGUAGE AND RACE

Now I turn to talk about the connections between social and rhetorical acts of naming languages within a hierarchy, and their connections with ethnic identity, race, and socioeconomic class. This topic was not fully developed in the data that I collected from my participants; rather, it is something I have since researched, once I realized that the categories of "stigma" and "race" required further investigation to understand the context for language use in this program. Overall, the participants in the two CSR program groups had very positive reviews of their time together. They enjoyed living and working together, and the local residents I interviewed felt that the visitors provided a great service in general medical care for the month that we were in town. Although I did not create interview protocol to specifically address the topic of race, it was present in daily discourse and my field notes. As I focused specifically on the thematic category of race, I also began to examine research on Dominican Spanish in the field of linguistics. This helped me develop a deeper understanding of stigma within linguistic hierarchies of Spanish.

The connections between languaging, national identity, and perceptions of ethnicity are important to consider in our rhetorical uptake of translanguaging. Talking about race and bodily features is very common in the Dominican Republic (and across Latin America), where common *apodos* (*nicknames*) or terms of endearment may be tied to complexion, such as moreno or prieto (*dark-skinned* or *black*), or someone might remind me how I used to be "más flaca o más gorda" (*thinner or fatter/bigger . . . in a healthy way*) last time he or she saw me. Although the majority of the visiting group would identify as white North Americans, there were a few participants who encountered other conversations about race and ethnicity. One of the medical students, Christina, and I had the following conversation about her need to respond to others' assumptions about her identity:

> RACHEL: Can you describe a time when you felt like you taught someone else about your own culture in the program?
> CHRISTINA: Yeah, I think so. Teaching people that I was not Chinese . . . So in the DR, and actually a lot of Latin America that I've experienced, if you're Asian, you're Chinese. And they would call me "China," and so I'd explain to them that I wasn't Chinese. I [am] actually Vietnam-

ese. It was interesting and it blew their mind that there was a country called Vietnam, and I don't think most people knew it was even on the map.
RACHEL: Really? Now we had another participant who was originally from Vietnam, right?
CHRISTINA: And he was "Chino."
RACHEL: Yeah, you both probably dealt with that a bit. Explaining or teaching them about that, right?
CHRISTINA: Yeah, and it was interesting because then they started teaching each other . . . I think some people started saying, "Oh, no no! She's not Chinese; she's from Vietnam" when they were saying that.

With these assumptions about ethnic identity also came assumptions about Christina's language abilities. Many children assumed she could speak Chinese. It was interesting to see how the time the children spent with Christina also turned into a learning experience about other Asian countries and the ethnicities of Americans.

Within the local context of the island of Hispaniola, race, language, and ethnicity are intertwined in discussions of Dominican identity, Dominican Republic–Haiti relations, and historical ties to Africa and native Taíno tribes. Although I do not have the space or data to report on the extremely complex and, at times, hostile relations between Dominican, Haitian, and Dominican Haitian individuals residing in the DR, I must acknowledge the social context within which we engaged in a "Dominican"[5] community. These interviews and notes are from 2011 and 2012, just before the infamous 2013 ruling by the Dominican Constitutional Court to denationalize over 250,000 immigrants and children born of immigrants from Haiti since 1929 (Rojas). In the communities we lived among, there were many individuals who were Haitian migrants, or very likely of Haitian descent. I observed segregation in the ways that many of them interacted, but also encountered friendly and familial relations among others. We were living in towns that were about a forty-five-minute drive to the border of Haiti; there were a number of Haitian or Dominican Haitian individuals who lived with us, helped us in the clinic, and came to be seen as patients in our clinics and friends outside of them. Some of them spoke fluent Spanish (among other languages) while others only spoke Haitian Creole and French.

The following is an excerpt from my field notes of June 27, 2012, which was the second day of clinic in Rancho de la Vaca:

> We have already had a few Haitian patients including one (dental patient) who didn't speak Spanish. That was really difficult/frustrating not being able to clearly communicate and make sure she understood what we were saying and doing . . . it made me nervous to work without any kind of translator (her mom spoke Spanish but she was in the medical part of the clinic when her daughter entered the dental). I asked [a Dominican helper] . . . what language the [patient] spoke and she said Haitiano, and I asked if she meant Creole, and she said yes.

The patient seemed to understand a little bit of Spanish, as demonstrated by her nonverbal responses to our questions when speaking to her in Spanish, and she nonverbally insisted that she wanted to do the extraction. Her mother was later able to join us, and we worked with the patient's intake form for information on her health history and reason for visiting the clinic. What stood out to me while reexamining my field notes, though, was how the Dominican helper said that the language the patient spoke was Haitiano (*Haitian*). Though the ayudante could have been shortening Haitian Creole when speaking to me, the association of language use with nationality and race was clearly a part of how this patient was "othered" within our Spanish-speaking Dominican context.

Perceptions of language are closely related to ideologies about race and culture. In Bullock and Toribio's research on Cibaeño Spanish, one interviewee specifically mentions one of the towns in my study as having an especially "bad" form of Spanish in relation to its Haitianized influence: "Por aquí . . . había una descendencia haitiana; en esa area . . . no se hablaba bien el español. 'Here . . . there was some Haitian heritage; in that area . . . people didn't speak

Spanish well.' (Middle class male; age 55)" ("Kreyol" 180). Bullock and Toribio explain that this town "is the smallest, least populated, and most rural of the towns [in their study], and it is commonly believed by other *fronterizos* to be a village settled by people of *descendencia haitiana*. 'Haitian descent'" (181). They explain that the popular view is that the "best" variety of Spanish is based on a European norm and the "worst" is spoken by Dominicans believed to have African heritage, which is a way to emphasize Dominicans' "hispanidad" while racializing Haitians. Bullock and Toribio's study demonstrates that Dominicans discriminate among varieties of Spanish from the Cibao region: "They ascribe low prestige to the speech of those whom they judge to be *campesinos*, that is, rural Dominicans. However, although they also *believe* these speakers to be of African descent from their speech forms, our results show that the judges could not accurately guess the skin color of the speakers" (189–90). These assumptions were related to class, education level, and African Haitian heritage. Their study concluded that "the linguistic traits that Dominicans stigmatize as 'Haitianized' properties are actually features of the speech of rural, uneducated *cibaeños* of all racial designations" (195). Therefore, the stigma placed on this form of Spanish has both racial and socioeconomic implications.

The language ideologies at play with these sorts of linguistic structures are what Flores and Rosa describe as "raciolinguistic ideologies." They argue that

> the ideological construction and value of standardized language practices are anchored in what we term *raciolinguistic ideologies* that conflate certain racialized bodies with linguistic deficiency unrelated to any objective linguistic practices. That is, raciolinguistic ideologies produce racialized speaking subjects who are constructed as linguistically deviant even when engaging in linguistic practices positioned as normative or innovative when produced by privileged white subjects. (150)

In this context, privileged white subjects included those with this identity in the Dominican Republic, the United States, and other Spanish-speaking countries. Understanding how raciolinguistic ideologies influence cross-cultural interactions illuminates the necessary rhetorical work of translanguaging to challenge linguistic inequality. Not only were my US participants learning to navigate Spanish in a context where globally, the local dialect would be considered low prestige, but also, the region we were in added the dimension that "whiter" individuals from middle and upper classes or other regions of the Dominican Republic would consider the local dialect to be a bad form of Spanish because of raciolinguistic ideologies. However, within this study, to acquire characteristics of this dialect was seen as speaking Spanish like a Dominican. To speak Spanish like a Dominican signified rhetorical adaptability and successful communication with patients. Therefore, the rural dialect of Dominican Spanish became the privileged discourse of our medical setting, and other "formal" versions of Spanish were perceived as needing translation.

The global frame of the low prestige of this dialect did influence some of the participants' judgments about the language and their inability to understand it at first. However, participants with limited proficiency saw it as "the way to speak Spanish," and those who may have placed judgment on the dialect still performed it at times in order to ease understanding and negotiate differences better. If I had conducted this study in any other context, any one of these variables could have changed. Understanding the layers of complexity within this specific context helps us better understand the distinctly rhetorical acts that participants used to privilege a form of Spanish that is not privileged in traditional linguistic hierarchies. The rhetoric of translanguaging interrogates stigma placed on varieties of languages and how individuals negotiate those differences across situated cultural and national contexts.

"KNOWING SPANISH"

From the perspective of the Dominican interviewees, US visitors either knew how to speak Spanish or did not. There were a few individuals who worked alongside the visitors in the clinics and who could identify the differences in Spanishes, but they often referred to these as differences in "accent." Within this specific context en los campos del Rancho de la Vaca and Buena Vista, if someone did not speak Spanish in a way that reflected the discursive qualities of the local dialect, he or she was viewed as someone who did not know Spanish very well and needed an interpreter. Rosa, a cooperadora de salud, explains:

> Vamo(s) decir, uno habla con esa gente que no entienden el español, si no le(s) entiendo, uno lo hace seña para que ello(s) lo pueden entender y si veamo(s) que no le entienden, entonce(s) no(s) va . . . donde la coordinadora de ello(s) porque entiende el español. Entonces nos le dice a la directora de ello(s) entonce(s) ella va a explicar al médico, o a la persona que nosotro(s) necesitamo(s) ella nos va a la clarafición. (*Let's say, [when] one speaks with these people that do not understand Spanish, if I do not understand them, one makes signals so that they can understand and if we see that they do not understand, then we go . . . where their coordinator is because she understands Spanish. So we say it to their director and then she can go explain to the doctor, or to the person that we need her to make the clarification for us.*)

In this quote, both coordinadora and directora are terms referring to me as the coordinator of the group. Rosa explains that they would turn to me to help translate for interactions with visitors who did not understand Spanish. It is possible that certain individuals knew some Spanish, or a different dialect of Spanish pretty well, but when faced with a conversational context in these towns, they appeared to not know Spanish and often needed interpretive assistance. Many of the Dominican interviewees cited how I helped interpret whenever they had an issue with understanding; although I often interpreted between English and Spanish, sometimes all I did was re-articulate what someone had said in Spanish in an accent, or rephrase to reflect the intonation and cadence of the local dialect. My ability to do this developed over the time I spent in the communities and the country. Disregarding national or hierarchical classifications of Spanish, the dialect of Spanish that I wanted to become fluent in was a form that these communities would recognize and that I could easily understand when they spoke to, and around, me.

In the following conversation, Daniel, a Dominican ayudante, explains to me how the differences in Spanish affected patient understanding in the clinic.

> DANIEL: Mi experiencia fue que había muchas personas en la clínica que no entendían lo que decían ustede(s). (*My experience was that there were many people in the clinic that did not understand what it was that you all said.*)
> RAQUEL: Y cuando ellos hablaron y los pacientes no entendieron, ¿estaban hablando en español? (*And when they spoke and the patients did not understand, were they [the Americans] speaking in Spanish?*)
> DANIEL: Sí, hablaban en español, pero los dominicano(s) no entendían bien. Entonce(s) yo le explicaba como era. (*Yes, they spoke in Spanish, but the Dominicans did not understand it well. So, I explained how it was.*)

Daniel and the other Dominican ayudantes quickly proved they understood the US participants' Spanish usage more easily than the clinic's visitors did. Because patients struggled to understand the practitioners' language use, it was immensely helpful to have younger volunteers in the clinic who were able to adjust between the Spanish of the patients and the Spanish of the US participants. By working with each other and spending time together, Dominican ayudantes were able to familiarize themselves with the visiting participants' languaging and the medical terminology used in the clinics. This led to a useful approach in which the Dominican ayudantes served as ad hoc interpreters when patients and practitioners were unable to achieve mutual understanding between their differing dialects of Spanish.

Additionally, the following excerpt from my field notes on July 13, 2012, shows when I first began to grapple with how to describe the ways that differences in accent and dialect influenced provider-patient interactions in the clinics.

I asked Juan and Ana what they thought about . . . how Matthew or the pharmacists could say something—and say it accurately in Spanish, but the patient wouldn't understand it and need one of them or me to say it again more clearly or in an accent they could understand. Ana explained it might just be that "nosotros estamos más acostumbrados a este acento que cuando uds hablan" (*we are more accustomed to this accent than when you all speak*). They then gave examples where they saw Matthew & Joshua experience that—mentioning the words *hepatitis* [that people thought was] (apetito) (*appetite*) & *embarazada* [that one person thought was] (envenenada) (*poisoned*) and there have been numerous other examples like this.

Juan and Ana laughed at these examples and the things the patients thought the US ayudantes had said. Even though these moments might have provided comic relief amid our hot and stressful workdays, they undoubtedly caused confusion for patients and challenged the ethos of our medical team. Having the Dominican ayudantes paired up with US ayudantes helped to quickly resolve these small moments of confusion, because someone would be close by to rephrase or re-state questions from the patient history form in a manera (*way*) that the patient would recognize. I will explore this form of translation more in the next chapter to examine how collective approaches to translanguaging can be fostered in translation spaces.

The rhetoric of translanguaging challenges linguistic inequality by complicating language ideologies. Raciolinguistic ideologies can lead to the marginalization of certain speakers based on their actual or perceived race and social status. However, if the goal of a program is to provide healthcare to a community, then the language used to discuss health and illness must reflect the discourse of that community. The members of this healthcare team decided, or were forced, to privilege the local Spanish dialect in their interactions and moments of translation, thus challenging power relations of the clinic. In this specific context, the ability to acquire speech habits of the local community was highly valued because this was the form of Spanish that could ensure understanding and develop rapport with patients and host families. As I explore in the next chapter, in this specific context, other "good" accents or dialects received blank looks and questions. Even if a healthcare provider considered the local language to have "improper grammar," many still tried to integrate aspects of the dialect into their Spanish because of its usefulness in this context. The providers learned to let go of grammatical rules and notions of "standard Spanish" to translanguage in more fluid and meaningful ways. Ultimately, examining rhetorical translanguaging within this context recognizes how situated practice affects whether a way of speaking is considered good, bad, or useful.

Built on an interrogation of linguistic inequality, the rhetoric of translanguaging complicates simplistic notions of translation by cultivating translation spaces across modes, languages, and discourses. Through moments of rephrasing, re-articulating, and interpreting languages, individuals who work together can uncover the complexity and layered nature of translation spaces. Although written texts are often used as languaging resources, they may be taken up in different ways if there is dissonance among various communal and institutional discourses. In the next chapter, I examine how some of my participants learned to negotiate written documents in response to patients' languaging about health and illness. By using a form of Spanish-to-Spanish interpretation with the Dominican ayudantes and negotiating written texts in the clinics, these participants took a rhetorical approach to translanguaging that can inform new approaches to medical translation spaces.

4

Cultivating Translation Spaces

TRANSLATION IS WHAT INDIVIDUALS TURN TO WHEN they are trying to understand languaging that is not easily recognizable within their existing linguistic repertoire. It is the work of bridging meaning across language variation and is often seen as simply transferring meaning from one language to another—whatever *that* means now that we've complicated what a language is or if any languages are distinctly one thing or another. For this chapter, I use Laura Gonzales and Rebecca Zantjer's definition of "translation" as "how individuals who speak more than one language convey the meaning of specific words across languages" (273), with the acknowledgment that the phrase "across languages" can include dialects of a named language. As I mentioned in Chapter 1, I define a translation space as any space that requires some type of translation work across different forms of meaning making through various modes, languages, and discourses. This perspective on translation also integrates textual spaces as written and spoken discourses are mediated and as texts are transformed through conversation. Therefore, translation spaces serve as contexts where language users negotiate across different modes (spoken-written, verbal-nonverbal), languages (English-Spanish, Spanish-Spanish), and institutional and communal discourses (provider-patient discourses of health). At any time, the collective language users may negotiate varied forms of each of these. The complexity of how my participants negotiated these various factors surfaced in their work with patient health history forms, oral consultations in the dental and medical clinics, and conversations with patients about medications and discharge instructions. By cultivating spaces where this negotiation was encouraged—and necessary—various team members took on the roles of ad hoc interpreters to translanguage across dialects and accents of varied Spanishes, to negotiate written and spoken words, and to respond to dissonance between medical Spanishes of providers and patients.

In medical settings, professional translators and interpreters do important work that helps marginalized speakers of certain languages obtain access to, and be understood by, speakers of the dominant language of whatever institutional space they inhabit. Translators make health documents more accessible to a wider variety of individuals who have difficulty reading the dominant language in which the materials are written. Considering audience and purpose, we can look at the role of the medical interpreter in three major ways: (1) she or he serves as a bridge between healthcare providers and patients; (2) she or he serves the healthcare provider as a client to transmit important medical information to patients who do not understand the provider's language use; and (3) she or he serves the patient to ensure that the healthcare provider understands the patient's needs and experiences. Interpreters serve in all of these capacities and more, but the final role is the one I am most interested in: how interpreters may translanguage in ways that negotiate power differentials within liminal spaces of translation to advocate for patients' needs and experiences.

The roles of interpreters in the United States have been examined to determine whether interpreters should act as an invisible conduit of language, a cultural broker, a collaborator, or an agent who intervenes in other ways (Hsieh; Dawson Estrada, Reynolds, and Hilfinger Messias; White and Laws). Within this study, my discussion of interpreters and interpreting refers to individuals who became ad hoc interpreters or who might be considered untrained or nonprofessional interpreters. Although there are many ethical issues with having medical interpretation conducted by untrained interpreters, this ad hoc nature of interpreting is common in transnational programs. People take on the interpreter roles based on their general language ability (or native fluency) and often negotiate medical terminology throughout their interactions with providers and patients. My data was able to capture the unique qualities of cross-dialectal and multimodal (Shipka) interpreting because of this ad hoc nature of interpretation. Individuals were responding to language variation in ways that necessitated the reliance on collective linguistic resources that might have been different with the presence of professionally trained medical interpreters. From a rhetorical perspective, interpretation that privileges communal discourses serves as an ethical step toward ensuring mutual understanding and advocacy on behalf of the patient within transnational healthcare.

Most people are familiar with the term "translation" and use it to describe a variety of interpretive acts. Translanguaging is not as commonly recognized or understood, either inside or outside of the academic community. Even the difference between interpretation (for speaking) and translation (for writing) is not always a defining aspect of how people use these terms in everyday discourse. In my study, the words "translate" and "translator" were used most often to describe interpret and interpreter. Therefore, when I interchange the words and talk about the multiple layers of translation spaces, it is based on my participants' constant exchange between written texts and oral discourse. In this chapter, I highlight how the rhetoric of translanguaging cultivates translation spaces that bring attention to various modes, languages, and discourses in translation work. Looking at language negotiation as translanguaging also illuminates how there are a variety of verbal and nonverbal tactics used to make connections across difference. Ultimately, a rhetoric of translanguaging within medical translation would privilege learning from the linguistic repertoires of patients and their communities to influence the dominant discourse of clinical interactions.

At first, translation spaces may look like a series of translation moments. According to Gonzales and Zantjer, translation moments are instances in time when multilingual communicators who are working across languages pause to make a rhetorical decision about how to translate a particular word or phrase from one language to another. In a translation space, when a communicator does this, she or he also analyzes the listener's verbal and nonverbal expressions to recognize when they have found common ground to understand the topic at hand. Sometimes a translation space entails negotiation back and forth between individuals to figure out what they want to discuss and how they can explain concepts to each other. To navigate translation moments, interpreters draw on a wide array of rhetorical strategies to contextualize language for their audiences, using intonation, gestures, and their cultural knowledge to make a rhetorical decision when selecting the language that will best inform their patient (Bloom-Pojar and Gonzales). Whereas understanding that translation moments examine an individual's perspective of rhetorical considerations when translating, looking at translation spaces allows us to observe the various actors participating in the translation-related activity and the modes, languages, and discourses they are negotiating together. These rhetorical decisions can lead to more multifaceted and ethical interactions between providers and patients when the shared linguistic repertoires of patients and translators are used. This leads to new approaches to translation in which we can recognize translation spaces as emerging among a variety of verbal and nonverbal rhetorical tactics.

WRITTEN-SPOKEN MEDICAL SPANISH TRANSLATION

In addition to encountering varieties of Spanishes in this context, certain participants who worked as interpreters struggled with translating between their medical Spanish and community discourses of health and illness. Because the language variation present among the healthcare team members complicated translation moments in the clinics, there were also moments of disconnect between what was recommended by various resources for medical Spanish and what was ultimately used for conversations with patients. These written resources were shared during orientation week and carried across contexts (from the United States to Santiago to clinics in the communities) to support translanguaging in the campo. Urciuoli explains how our sense of "correctness" in language use is related to these texts:

> The social process of imagining language as a system of linguistic forms, and attributing stability and correctness to those

forms, is in most contemporary societies shaped by the ways in which language practices are entextualized (Silverstein and Urban 1996) through metalinguistic publication, particularly those through which language standards are disseminated—dictionaries, reference grammars, [and] school texts. (260)

Talking about medical discourse in any "language" brings up questions about how words and phrases within what is the "same" named language can lead to the need to translate or explain in layperson's terms. For instance, simply because I am fluent in English does not mean I will understand all of the English words that my physician might use when describing a technical procedure or diagnosis. Similarly, just because our healthcare providers had studied and memorized medical Spanish terminology did not mean that those words would translate to the local ways of talking about symptoms and disease. If the visitors embarked on the trip with only one memorized form of describing certain symptoms or conditions, they were challenged in the clinics with situations in which they needed to rephrase or consider alternative words for what they were trying to say.

Notions of transfer further complicate translation spaces when translanguaging might be a better approach for moving across contexts. García and Wei argue that

> translanguaging allows us to shed the concept of *transfer* and to adopt a conceptualization of *integration* of language practices in *the person of the learner*.... Rather than learning a new separate "second language," learners are engaged in appropriating new languaging that makes up their own unique repertoire of meaning-making resources. The language practices then don't belong to the school or to the home; the languaging is that of the learner, his or her own being, knowing and doing, as it emerges through social interaction. (80)

Rather than focusing on the transfer of the language learned in their Spanish or medical Spanish classes, the US healthcare providers would have benefited from an understanding of how translanguaging emerges through social interaction. Preparation for transnational trips, as for CSR's program, often entail a circulation of texts: vocabulary lists, textbooks, PowerPoint presentations, and more to prepare the visitors for terms and phrases they should use and recognize while in the community. However, reliance on these texts is often disrupted when the individual realizes that the written words are not transferring to the spoken context she or he has entered. One of the major issues with these moments of disruption relates to individuals' reliance on notions of standard language use and professional medical terminology. When practitioners receive texts like these, it would be helpful for them to understand how the texts are based on a perceived standard that may need to be rephrased or discussed in completely different ways depending on local contexts and dialects. Rhetorical translanguaging provides a way to respond to this disconnect between written texts for language learning and transcultural medical settings.

In my analysis, the patient intake process was one of the areas where participants encountered the most disconnect between written texts and spoken words. The intake process is set up as a dialogue between the patient and an ayudante or nurse to facilitate the filling out of a patient health history form (see Figure 4) to prepare for the examination in either the dental or the medical side of the clinic. CSR provides these forms during orientation week, and group leaders inform the US ayudantes that the forms are to be used as aids for asking questions to document a patient's health history during the intake process. Anis Bawarshi explains how the patient medical health history form, as a genre, "helps organize and generate the social and rhetorical environments within which patients and doctors speak to one another" (Devitt, Bawarshi, and Rieff 551). Within CSR's program, these forms moved across the clinics as the patients brought them to the waiting area, the medical or dental consultation, and the pharmacy, and then left them to be used for potential follow-up or referrals within CSR. However, Andrew explains how some of the terminology did not translate when having conversations with the patients: "Some of the vocab that they have written out, the questions that we had to ask, were different from what . . . the patients would understand. . . . It was frustrating at times when . . . [you] have a question written for you, and you read it, and it's not being understood . . . [or] that you didn't know how else to ask it." The tension between the US ayudantes' oral articulation of written terminology and the patients' own discourses and understandings of what was said led to a need for alternative phrasing or translation work. Dominican and US ayudantes turned to each other for help in rephrasing questions, and they began to annotate the document with alternate words and questions to improve their performance with each patient interaction.

MEDICO						
Today's Date_____						
Nombres_____ Apellidos_____ Apodo_____						
Edad_____ Sexo_____ Fecha de Nacimiento (*day/month/year*)_____						
Número de teléfono_____-_____-_____						
Nacionalidad_____		Cédula_____				
Comunidad_____		Cooperador_____				

Tiene Usted una historia de:			Tiene Usted un problema con:			
Asma	Sí	No	Muchos Sangrados	Sí	No	
Problemas con respiración	Sí	No	Ataque o epilepsia	Sí	No	
Diabetes	Sí	No				
Enfermedad del riñón	Sí	No				
Fiebre reumática	Sí	No	Tiene Usted Alérgicos de:			
Enfermedad del corazón	Sí	No	Penicilina	Sí	No	
Anemia	Sí	No	Novocaina	Sí	No	
Enfermedad del hígado			Aspirina	Sí	No	
(Hepatitis)	Sí	No	Otra medicina o comida	Sí	No	
Presión Alta/Hipertensión	Sí	No	¿If sí, que?_____			

Para las mujeres:
  ¿Está Usted embarazada?   Sí   No   ¿If sí, cuantos meses?_____

Para toda la gente:
  ¿Usted sufre de alguna enfermedad?   Sí   No   ¿If sí, cuál?_____

  ¿Alguna vez Ud. ha sido atendido por
  un Operativo del ▓▓▓▓?   Sí   No   ¿If sí, cuál?_____
              CSR
  (If si) ¿Ud. recibió/tiene un numero de
  tarjeta del ▓▓▓▓?   Sí   No   If sí, Número:_____
              CSR

(For the nurse/med student/doctor)

Vitales: T_____ F or C   P_____ R_____ BP_____

Figure 4. Partial health history form (CSR 2011).

By rhetorically analyzing the partial health history form in Figure 4, we can assume that the audience for this written form is primarily an English-speaking doctor or healthcare team member, and secondarily, the patient or Spanish-speaking healthcare provider who might follow up on a referral for that patient. The primary audience might be inferred from the following: Today's Date is requested in English; English is also used for la fecha (day/month/year); there are multiple phrases that begin with If sí (If *yes*); and on the bottom of the form, it states, For the nurse/med student/doctor.

These instances reflect some of the translanguaging inherent in the conversations around the form, and its movement across the clinics from intake to the consultation to the pharmacy. Yoel, a Dominican ayudante, lists some of the questions that were the same for every patient: "Como: si sufría de diabetes; si sufría del corazón; si sufría del alguna otra enfermedad, y que se iba hacer como el odontología, si *a filling*, si empaste." (*Like: If you've suffered from diabetes, if you've suffered from the heart [heart disease]; if you've suffered from any other illness, and what they were going to do like dentistry, if a filling [in English], if filling.*) These examples show how ayudantes shortened formal terminology to reflect how the local residents discussed common health issues, such as asking, "Si sufría del corazón" instead of "Si sufría de la enfermedad del corazón." His mention of a filling at the end of his response also shows how Yoel had learned intake terminology in English: many times, the US ayudante would write the word "filling" in English so that the dentist knew what it was. The dental clinic form was different from the medical one in Figure 4, and these forms may have changed in the years since I collected data.

Certain questions on the medical intake form include the official terminology, such as ¿Tiene Usted una historia de diabetes? (*Do you have a history of diabetes?*), but the ayudantes learned that it was more common to ask, "¿Tiene azúcar?" (Literally, *Do you have sugar?*) or "¿Sufre del azúcar? (Literally, *Do you suffer from sugar?*) In our clinics, it also became important to recognize that when someone said, "Tengo azúcar," it meant *I have diabetes*. Because a similar phrase is also common in some English-speaking communities ("I've got the sugars"), this specific example indicates the importance of studying how and why people talk about their conditions and how these patient discourses of health can transfer to other contexts. Other terms on the form were more easily understood in an alternate phrasing, such as choosing presión alta in place of hipertensión, similar to how US English-speakers more commonly say "high blood pressure" in place of hypertension. These are just a few examples of the various ways that participants negotiated differences among written and spoken medical Spanishes as these discourses traveled from classrooms in specific US contexts to rural communities in the Dominican Republic.

Making the decision to change the phrasing of the intake form during a consultation requires a certain "reading of the patient" by recognizing moments of misunderstanding. In describing such moments, Andrew explains,

> In a clinical setting in which we've been in this program, I mean there's kind of a whole 'nother vocabulary there to learn with the medical Spanish, and so, and that's maybe some stuff that the campesinos don't know that vocab, and so having to explain stuff like that to them is difficult. . . . I think a lot of it is kind of reading facial expressions and body language and if you can sense they don't get it, asking, like "did you understand all that?" and then trying to . . . put it in, I don't know, more laymen's terms, so to speak.

When the US healthcare team initially encountered these vocabulary lists, they seemed to represent the "correct" way to discuss patient health histories. However, when healthcare team members tried to transfer their languaging knowledge from written resources to situated, local conversations, they encountered dissonance and learned that they would need to adjust their phrasing to communicate more effectively. By acknowledging how these words and phrases (what Andrew refers to as laymen's terms) belong to a complex discourse with high stakes for patient understanding, I refer to them as part of *patient* and *community discourses of health*. Community discourses of health represent terminology that is equally as important as the medical terms the practitioners learned in school. These discourses represent another set of phrases that the healthcare providers needed to learn and understand within a specific medical context. Many US ayudantes ended up keeping a copy of the form with handwritten notes about how to rephrase or ask questions in another way to reflect the local discourse. Much of that helped, but sometimes an ayudante's accent still inhibited the patient from understanding what exactly it was that he or she was asking. Regardless, the ways that CSR group leaders, ayudantes, and patients talked together using these forms transformed the ways the forms were used and articulated during the patient intake process.

Other texts that were transformed through dialogue were dictionaries and vocabulary lists of medical Spanish. Multiple US participants noted differences in the professional Spanish they learned in textbooks and classes versus the local, campo Spanish that was spoken in the region where they were living. Andrew explains, "Regardless of how much you study . . . Spanish . . . in classes or in textbooks, it's an entirely different situation to have to converse in it, especially with native speakers." When discussing difficulties with adjusting to Dominican Spanish, US participants often mentioned that it was very fast. One of my assistant coordinators, Jacob, explains, "I'm fluent in Spanish, but you have to really stop people, 'cause Dominican Spanish is very fast, very, very . . . [but] if you have the willingness to really slow people down and if the other person is really willing to listen to what you have to say, and meet you there, then from there, you can have a lot better communication." Additionally, Abby, a pharmacy student, explains how being someone with less proficiency in Spanish resulted in a complicated process of trying to implement learned language from the orientation week:

> They teach you terms in that class like that first week that we're there and then you try to remember them and implement them and they don't understand what you're saying. Like you could try to say in Spanish, "Please slow down," and

they don't know what you're saying, and then you feel foolish because you're trying to speak their language . . . you're like Por favor, lentamente, lentamente! [*Please, slowly, slowly!*] And they're like, *What?* [laughs].

What became difficult for speakers was when they would focus on accurately articulating vocabulary and phrases learned in the classroom, these words and phrases did not transfer to lived contexts in Rancho de la Vaca and Buena Vista. Also, visitors' comprehension was challenged by the local residents' speed and accent, and that made it more challenging to pick up dialectal features in relation to what the visitors learned in classes. In Abby's case, the local residents might use the phrase más despacio (*more slowly*) instead of the phrase that she cites. Lentamente could be considered technically correct in being translated as "slowly," but más despacio was used more often in this context when describing speech.

Many US participants took on the roles of ad hoc interpreters in addition to their designated roles as nurse, doctor, pharmacist, and others. As they took on these roles, they turned to medical dictionaries and written resources for reference while conversing with patients. Lisa describes the complex process that happened as she moved back and forth across languages while translating for a physician and patient:

> I was helping translate for our doctor, who was from Nepal, and then the patient who spoke Spanish . . . we struggled through it. I think a guy came in with a rash and he kept saying "Comí, Comí" which means like "I ate." And I was like, "But it's on your skin!" And I don't know . . . I just had an "aha" moment where "comí" is like rash is eating your skin . . . and then I had to look up the word for powder and then was trying to translate all of this between English to Spanish. It was kind of chaotic.

Patients often use metaphors to explain health issues, and this is important to understand when translating in a multilingual healthcare setting. Lisa was able to eventually move from a literal translation and misunderstanding toward making connections and helping support the physician in her diagnosis. Lisa also mentions that this process was chaotic and that she used a dictionary to aid in the process. The ultimate realization of what the patient was describing would not be easily found in her dictionary, though, and was instead pulled from her linguistic repertoire related to metaphors of discomfort (a rash "eating at" one's skin). Only through patience and the determination to work through this complexity in translation spaces could participants attempt to find that "aha" moment that Lisa describes.

In their chapter "Translingual Literacy and Matters of Agency," Lu and Horner explain that "a translingual approach defines languages not as something we have or have access to but as something we do. It centers attention on languaging: how we do language and why" (27). This definition resonates with the ways in which participants performed language by trying out new words and phrases that they learned from each other rather than memorizing them from print texts. Elizabeth, a nursing student, explains how she and the ayudantes would support each other's languaging in their downtime between patients: "Each of them spoke just like a little bit of English where we would try and teach them words, and they knew how to like talk slower [in Spanish], but we also would pull out our dictionaries sometimes . . . [and] I think they were just . . . a lot more understanding of the fact that we didn't speak fluent Spanish." With the aid of dictionaries, the ayudantes and nursing students set up a mutually beneficial relationship by teaching each other English and Spanish phrases as they worked together throughout the program. Joshua, who served as an ayudante, adds, "In a clinical setting, when I was just trying to learn words and phrases, I would work with the other ayudantes and just be like, 'How do I say, Stand here so I can measure you?' Or . . . just something very basic . . . and then they would ask me, 'How you say that in English?'" The moments of downtime that the ayudantes had together provided space and time for developing rhetorical strategies to translanguage. The US ayudantes and nursing students were able to develop their proficiencies in Spanish by having coworkers who understood their struggles with the language. Although dictionaries were used as an aid for dialogue, social interactions and gestures while working in the material context of the clinic truly enhanced US participants' ability to translanguage in new ways. Supporting each other's language development allowed them to serve the patients better in the clinics, and by using that time in between work with patients to learn from each other, the nursing students and the ayudantes also deepened their relationships with each other.

However, in order to see all of the patients who had been promised an appointment by the time the clinic was supposed to close each day, we could not allow everyone to just sit and struggle through languaging for long periods of time with each patient. Not only would this be inefficient, it could also harm the ethos of the provider as being able to help patients medically. Instead, the expansion and use of individuals' full linguistic repertoires most often occurred outside the clinical setting or during in-between moments when practitioners could take risks or spend time learning to language in ways that might help them more effectively communicate with patients and host families.

In these examples, texts such as dictionaries and vocabulary lists were transformed from static words and phrases to collaborative actions to build up each other's linguistic repertoires. This approach to translanguaging "shifts our focus away from individuals, located on a fixed scale of competence toward 'mastery' of a reified 'target' language, and toward groups of people working in collaboration to use all available linguistic resources" (Horner, NeCamp, and Donahue 288). Not only did these ayudantes and nursing students use dictionaries together, they also learned to ask questions in other ways than what was written down for them to memorize and recite. The transformation from written texts to dynamic dialogues was possible only because of the translation spaces they cultivated through translanguaging together in their moments of downtime. Ultimately, their shared goal of helping patients served as a motive to improve subsequent interactions with each other and with their patients.

ENGLISH-SPANISH INTERPRETATION

The most basic and common use of oral interpretation in this study could be found with individuals who were able to move back and forth between English and Spanish, drawing from their full linguistic repertoire with ease. Katy explains that whenever she could not understand what someone said, she would go "buscar la coordinadora y decirle 'Ohh, no entiendo que me dice. ¿Podría explicarme sobre de lo que me hablan?' O, por ejemplo, cuando iban personas para consultar y le decíamos 'Ay, tengo un dolor de cabeza,' y ellos quizá(s) no entendían, pues la coordinadora le explicaba y también le explicaba a nosotros en español lo que ellos decían" (*to look for the coordinator and to say to her, "Ohh, I don't understand what she or he's saying to me. Could you explain to me what they're talking about?" Or, for example, when people went for their consultation and we said "Ay, I have a headache," and they perhaps didn't understand, but the coordinator explained to them and also explained to us in Spanish what they said*). Katy describes how she would approach my assistant coordinator or me to ask for an explanation any time that she did not understand what someone was saying or the physicians did not understand what a patient was saying. Many times a translator was nearby, but on the occasions when I (or another translator) was with another provider and patient, this added a delay to the communication between parties in the clinic.

Abby also describes the challenges of having someone translate for her in this specific clinical setting: "It was a little odd because you really can't talk normally when you have somebody translate because you have to stop every few words until it's translated and then pick up again. And a lot of the time I had forgotten the point of what I was trying to make." Abby's description demonstrates how translation is unique to this temporary clinical setting and may be different from other institutional settings. Because the interpreters in the clinic were not trained medical interpreters, they often needed to stop every few words or sentences in order to ensure an accurate interpretation. This resulted in longer interactions when interpretation was needed, especially when interpreters needed additional clarification about medical terminology in English from the practitioner or in Spanish from patients.

The differences in professional versus communal medical terminology in Spanish and English also required strategies that would disrupt the normal flow of interpretation. Since we did not staff the clinics with trained medical interpreters, differences in terminology required tactics of slowing down, defining terms, and alternating eye contact between the patient and the interpreter. Thus, when using English-Spanish interpretation, it was important that all parties involved understood the technical terminology in the conversation. At times, our healthcare providers would need to translate medical terminology across Englishes so that the translator could explain it in Dominican Spanish. Nicole, a dental student, explains:

> In the dental school we're taught [that] . . . it is best to make eye contact directly with the patient and not the translator. So the translator is a third person and you need to directly communicate with the patient. But, in [this setting in] the Dominican Republic it's hard because the translators don't know the words or know the entire phrase that we're trying to say in their language . . . it was a lot more one-on-one communication with the translator and then the translator with the patient, versus me talking to the patient and having it translated.

Describing the back-and-forth that healthcare providers need to have with their translators before even transferring the information to the patient demonstrates the complicated negotiation that takes place in the clinics. Both Spanish- and English-speaking participants mentioned the need to ask someone to slow down in order to understand better, and the need for patience in frustrating situations of misunderstanding.

Serving as an interpreter in these clinics reflected Canagarajah's description of translanguaging as the "ability of multilingual speakers to shuttle between languages, treating the diverse languages that form their repertoire as an integrated system" ("Codemeshing" 401). This shuttling requires various forms of internal and external translation. When describing his experience as a member of the team that could shuttle between English and Spanish, Andrew explains that "it's exhausting . . . when you switch and you're always constantly having to think in Spanish and figuring out what it means in English, and then formulate your response in Spanish . . . it's tiring going back and forth like that." For many of these participants, this was one of the first times that they needed to constantly shuttle between languages in a professional setting. The additional need to help other members of the group understand Spanish conversations increased the pressure for individuals who could more easily translanguage to constantly be prepared to interpret for someone else. Joshua adds that he felt the US participants "who spoke Spanish so well . . . [they] had no trouble speaking Spanish and then turning it off and then speaking English with us. I think the people who don't speak as good Spanish really appreciate that because we know you're doing twice the amount of speaking that we are, [laughs] . . . at least." Referring to the bilingual conversations that the group would have and the constant interpretation he observed, Joshua acknowledges that the language work for these individuals was at least twice as intense as for those who needed the interpretation. While a seemingly obvious observation, acknowledging the emotional and material components of engaging in this type of translanguaging is important. By understanding what challenges individuals in moments of translanguaging and translation with others, we can better explore what conditions help them persevere through those moments.

Though my own healthcare literacy among Spanishes and Englishes developed through participation with these programs, there were still moments when I would have to ask for clarification of diseases, medications, or follow-up procedures to ensure that I was translating them properly for the patients. This happened with other interpreters as well, since the team represented a wide variety of specialties and disciplinary backgrounds. Additionally, because many of the US participants served in some capacity as interpreters at one point or another, unique dynamics emerged with the varied ways that each spoke Spanish. This required interpretive assistance from the Dominican ayudantes, who were the most familiar with the local dialect of Spanish and community discourses of health.

SPANISH-SPANISH INTERPRETATION

Translanguaging allows us to see the complexity of translation in that it does not just occur across two separate codes or named languages, and it emphasizes how interpreters draw from their full linguistic repertoire. The Dominican ayudantes noticed that patients seemed to have trouble understanding the accent of the visiting providers, so they stepped in to help as interpreters and cultural brokers between the healthcare providers and patients. All of the US participants in this study tried to speak Spanish in the clinic, whether it was with a few words and pointing or attempting to hold entire conversations. There were multiple layers of Spanish translation, re-articulation, and pronunciation happening at any given time. Through these occurrences, a type of Spanish-Spanish interpretation emerged in the translation spaces of daily clinic activities. Yoel, one of the Dominican ayudantes, explains, "Yo le ayudaba a traducirle a todo los pacientes. . . . A veces de inglés a español y de español a español. . . . Porque no estaban impuestos a escuchar a esa lengua—escuchar la manera de hablar de los americanos." (*I helped translate for all the patients. . . . Sometimes from English to Spanish and sometimes from Spanish to Spanish. . . . Because they [the patients] were not used to listening to this language—listening to the way the Americans speak.*) From my first analysis of the data, this Spanish-Spanish interpretation, as Yoel describes it, became one of the most interesting findings, and it now serves as one of the most illuminating examples of rhetorical translanguaging in translation.

I also realized that part of our Spanish-Spanish languaging issues occurred when the patients were a bit older, which led to certain Dominican ayudantes serving as intergenerational language brokers (Alvarez) in these translation spaces. In my conversation with Miguel during his interview, he explained that he sometimes needed to use a simpler Spanish when interpreting for older patients:

> RAQUEL: Y ustedes ayudaban con [la explicación de] cosas que . . . como por ejemplo alguien [habló] en español pero . . . algunos pacientes no entendieron el español de los americanos?

(*And you all helped with [the explanation of things] that . . . like for example someone [spoke] in Spanish but . . . some patients did not understand the Spanish of the Americans?*)

MIGUEL: Algunos entendían pero siempre había alguien que le podía . . . interpretaba má(s) fácil lo que ello(s) decían y le explicaba. Personas anciana que están . . . no interpretaban bien, pues tenemos este problema que no sabían bien . . . no entendían bien lo, por su—no escuchaban bien. Y entonce(s) le explicaba—había otro que le explicaba como un español más . . . más simple para ellos. (*Some understood but there was always someone who could . . . interpret more simply what they said and explain it. Elderly people who are . . . who don't interpret well, well we have this problem that they do not know . . . they do not understand well the, for their—they do not hear well. And so, I explained it like [in] a Spanish that's more . . . that's simpler for them.*)

I kept Miguel's processing of how to describe what was happening in the quotation from his interview to demonstrate the difficulty that much of the healthcare team had in describing why patients did not understand the US participants' use of Spanish. His description demonstrates the complexity of reflecting on the various factors that influence patient communication and understanding in clinical settings: hearing ability, comprehension, health literacy, familiarity with accent, and more. Although he may also have been trying to remain respectful to his elders, Miguel ends his comment with the claim that they did not hear well, but then he goes on to say that he or others would explain in a simpler Spanish for them. Simplifying the complicated or mispronounced Spanish of the US participants was one of the many tactics these Spanish-Spanish interpreters used to translate across Spanishes.

There were also moments when the Dominican *ayudantes* helped with interpretation if the healthcare providers knew only some words in Spanish and said others in English when trying to articulate prescription directions or questions for the patients. Daniel describes one experience when he stepped in to help with interpreting in the pharmacy: "Yo recuerdo que hubo una señora que le estaban explicando cómo debía tomarse lo(s) medicamento(s), y ella no entendía. Entonce(s) yo . . . les dije que me explicaran a mí para yo explicárselo a ella. . . . Me lo decía(n) en español, pero decía(n) palabras en inglés que yo le entendía." (*I remember that there was a woman to whom they were explaining how to take the medications, and she did not understand. So . . . I told them to explain to me so I could explain it to her. They told me in Spanish, but [also] said words in English that I understood.*) Ensuring that patients understand discharge instructions and how to take their medications was very important. With so many sections of the clinic needing language support, it was helpful to have ayudantes like Daniel who could understand both English and Spanish. Although a few of the Dominican ayudantes understood English, they mainly used it for helping with interpretation in these translation spaces. These skills were especially helpful when US participants tried speaking Spanish but still inserted English prepositions or words when they did not know the Spanish terms to use. In these instances, Dominican ayudantes helped rearticulate sentences to be completely in Spanish.

For US participants, the Dominican volunteers and their Spanish-Spanish interpretation were crucial to the success of the clinic. Elizabeth explains, "The first week in clinic was really difficult doing intake, because I just kept getting super tongue-tied every time I tried to ask something and . . . they would just look at me . . . then like my Dominican ayudante helper would translate and they'd eventually get it." When describing the process, Elizabeth explained that "they [the ayudantes] would kind of . . . slow things down for us or speed things up the other way around . . . it helped the gap a little bit even though they still spoke Spanish. It was good . . . translating my Spanish into faster Dominican Spanish and vice versa." Seeing the success of pairing up Dominican ayudantes with nursing students and US ayudantes for the patient intake process during my first year with the program, I began the second summer with the plan to set up the clinic similarly.

I asked the Dominican ayudantes to be available to help with interpretation, but to allow the US participants to try to speak Spanish first and encourage them to learn to converse with patients on their own. Lisa argues that the Dominican ayudantes

> were the biggest asset to us. Like, they helped us out more than *anyone* with the language barrier . . . they allowed us to try to speak Spanish to the patient, and then once the patient was like, "I have no clue." They would repeat it in Spanish and it would sound the exact same thing like I said, but the patient would get it.

Many US participants mentioned feeling as if the Dominican ayudantes would say "the same thing" but just in a different accent or with a few different endings on words. Whether they were re-stating phrases, or reformulating a set of words into a full sentence, the ayudantes' help with translation in the clinic was clearly a crucial component to making it run smoothly.

Multiple US participants were not even sure whether they should call this process "interpretation" or "translation" since it was all within the same language of Spanish. However, they continued to refer to it as translation or interpretation because that was what it most resembled in the clinic: a third party accompanied the provider or ayudante and patient and helped re-articulate what was said on each side to ease the conversation and understanding between them. Ultimately, they were all drawing on their full linguistic repertoires in any way they knew how, but the additional translation work (rephrasing, re-articulating, and adding onto) of the Dominican ayudantes helped to cultivate translation spaces across linguistic differences in their various dialects of Spanish.

Paul, a medical student, reflects on instances when he encountered this form of Spanish-Spanish interpretation: "I'm not sure if it was a language thing or if it was an accent thing, but there were definitely a couple of times that I had patients who would voluntarily yell outside of the room for . . . one of our Dominican helpers to come and interpret, which was really just kind of [to] repeat what I said in Spanish, but in a different accent, which was the first that I've ever had that as a quote-unquote 'interpreter.'" When this occurred within the medical examination room, it became complicated. Paul and other interpreters already available would try to encourage the patient to work through the language difference with them so that they could try to resolve the issue and not involve too many people from outside of their exam room. However, if trying to negotiate the language difference did not work after a few attempts, they turned to either an ayudante or one of the coordinators to help facilitate the conversation. By describing times when a patient would yell for a Dominican ayudante to come and help, Paul also reveals a reversal of roles in the clinic by privileging the expertise and skills of the young adult from the community who could speak and comprehend the languaging of the patient and the provider. The provider's status and control over the situation was challenged because his or her information was meaningless if the patient did not understand it. This also represents a moment when Paul's authority was challenged because his Spanish, although professional, was perceived as needing translation.

Other team members saw this use of Dominican ayudantes as interpreters to be the key to efficient information transfer. When describing the Spanish-Spanish translation help he received, Joshua explains that having Pedro re-articulate questions was "way faster, especially when we were asking for what they were allergic to, it was like Pe-ni-ci-lina, No-vo-caína, As-pirina, and I'd say it like that and then Pedro would just rattle it off in a second and they'd be like, 'Oh, oh, no no no.'" Not only did this use of Spanish-Spanish interpretation help improve efficiency with the patient intake process, but it also promoted the ethos of the clinic as a whole. When the first interaction a patient has with the clinic is a long, drawn-out process where the US volunteer is struggling to communicate, the credibility and quality of the rest of the visit may be in question. By collaborating as a team to prepare patients for visits to the medical or dental clinic, the ayudantes boosted the entire clinical team's credibility as one that could communicate effectively in a multilingual environment.

In my field notes on July 13, 2012, I reflected on instances when I did a similar form of Spanish-Spanish interpretation with others in the pharmacy and patient intake station:

> It's been interesting interpreting today, especially in the pharmacy where oftentimes the pharmacy students can explain instructions in Spanish fine (Toma 1 tableta dos veces cada dia) [*Take 1 tablet two times a day*] but sometimes patients won't understand them and then I say the same thing (with more of a local accent) and they get it. [I'm curious about] the difference an accent (which I've developed the past couple years) can make in the understanding/reception of Spanish spoken here. I just asked Matthew "Why do you think accents make such a big difference in understanding someone else?" and he said he wonders that every day when people ask him to repeat things or have Ana say the same thing.

While working through this project and during my time in the country, I was not sure what term to use: dialect, accent, variety, or something else. What I knew was that it did relate to *how* people phrased things. Their intonation, cadence, and markers of dialect influenced patient understanding. I also believe that part of the need for repetition came from the Dominican patient not expecting the foreign provider to speak Spanish. I encountered many times when someone asked me to repeat myself because it appeared as though they had not expected Spanish to come out of my mouth, and thus they had missed what I said.

Other participants who were less proficient in Spanish did not see the Spanish-Spanish translation as just a restatement of a question with a different accent. Nicole describes her own attempts at Spanish in the clinic:

> The first verb should be conjugated; I would not conjugate it. . . . I don't know if nouns can be in the wrong tense, but it probably was. . . . This one time Pedro kind of was just standing there next to me, and he turned to the patient and he changed all the words, but I could tell that they were the

same words; they just had different endings. The patient nodded their head. . . . It was translating my Spanish to better Spanish.

Noticing that Pedro was adjusting the grammatical structure of her sentences by changing the endings of words was a unique observation among her peers in the program. Nicole worked to learn more Spanish each week that she was in the campo and was very attuned to grammatical structure while speaking, as many beginning-level Spanish learners are in the United States. Drawing from coursework that emphasized how to conjugate verbs, but also not always catching everything that was said in Spanish, Nicole saw this translation as a move to improve her Spanish. Even in a theoretical sense of standard language, Pedro was probably "correcting her grammar" to reflect a standard use of Spanish, but I also imagine that some of the words he used or ways that he phrased things were built on his conversational fluency in the local dialect. In this context, the local dialect and pronunciation was the most useful form of the language, and thus the participants considered the ability to speak it as being skilled at communicating during the program.

The participants also engaged in a type of rhetorical attunement (Lorimer Leonard) to adjust their speech habits. Paul explains how he would adjust his languaging to try to help with the language difference: "I use more of a Spaniard Spanish type accent . . . and because of that, there were definitely times when I would say a word or a phrase that I realized from the patient's blank face that I needed to repeat in a different way or try to make sound more Dominican . . . usually when I'd try to do that, we were able to communicate well enough." Even though Paul and others with more advanced proficiency in Spanish felt that they had said a sentence correctly, the patients still responded better to discussions of their health and symptoms in their own dialect, their own *correct* way of speaking. This move to translanguage in ways that re-articulated the healthcare providers' use of Spanish to reflect the discourses of the patients was rhetorical. It challenged linguistic hierarchies and status within a professional, medical space by privileging the needs and languaging of the patient and local community. By having ayudantes help rephrase sentences or healthcare providers adjust their languaging over time to "sound more Dominican," the healthcare team took a rhetorical approach to cultivating translation spaces in our clinics. They began to translanguage in ways that privileged the speech habits of their patients and adjusted, or translated, their Spanish into a form that reflected the community discourses.

NONVERBAL-VERBAL TACTICS

The rhetorical uses of nonverbal tactics and body language for communication are also important for understanding translanguaging in translation spaces. The dental clinic provided an interesting site for studying nonverbal tactics since most of the participants who worked as dentists were less proficient in Spanish. Additionally, in contrast to medical consultations where the majority of their interactions consisted of verbal exchanges, dentists identified oral issues by looking at the mouth, and that visual was supplemented with a description of the pain and purpose of the visit. Within these clinics, dental visits could have only one of three procedures: cleaning, filling, or extraction. The majority of the dialogue between dentists and patients was at the beginning of the appointment to determine what type of pain the patient had and for how long. Then throughout the procedure, there was a set of commands that the dentists had learned from orientation, such as *bite down, spit, open,* and *show me where it hurts.*

Peter describes his encounters with Spanish as being easier inside the dental clinic than outside it. He explains: "It was definitely a lot easier in the clinic 'cause at least in the clinic, I knew dental terms and things related to dentistry and the mouth, but when conversational Spanish—I mean they could be talking about anything or asking me anything and so that made it a lot harder." Peter adds, "Inside the dental clinic was a little bit easier 'cause . . . you're dealing with one part, so if you ask, 'Are you in pain?' and they say, 'Sí,' I mean you can have them open up their mouth and have a pretty good idea of where they're at." I spent most of my time interpreting within the dental clinic and also noticed that the dentists often accompanied words with actions such as pointing to different areas of the mouth, physically demonstrating how to bite down or spit, and showing children how the instruments would not hurt them by tapping the tool on their own fingers and saying, "No duele." (*It doesn't hurt.*)

Participants with little to no proficiency in Spanish provided some of the most detailed descriptions of how to use nonverbal tactics in communicating. Nicole explains, "I think across nations, we communicate very much through facial expressions, body motions, and nonverbal cues. And in the Dominican Republic, I think I saw a lot more nonverbal communication through action . . . through just eye contact and motioning to try to get a point across." Nicole's emphasis on bodily cues demonstrates the importance of nonverbal tactics in one's linguistic repertoire. Translanguaging in practice inherently includes aspects of embodied, nonverbal communication; investigating it in this health communication context further emphasizes the importance of understanding and learning its role and potential for rhetorical acts in clinical settings.

Within the medical clinic, the consultations were almost entirely verbal exchanges and thus required creative rhetorical tactics to overcome not knowing a word or phrase. Alexis, one of my assistant coordinators, explains it this way:

> I would be helping translate for a physician and a patient wouldn't understand like a symptom I was trying to describe or I wouldn't be able to understand some sort of illness that they were describing to me, and it . . . really challenges the creative side of you because you have to come up with different ways to say things or use body language to help describe, so I think that language barrier really forces you to think outside the box.

Identifying body language as a useful tool for describing symptoms was a common theme for participants in this part of the clinic. Christina, a medical student, specifically notes hand gestures as something that helped in her consultations with patients: "If I asked, 'Well, do you have any headaches? Abdominal pain?' I'd point to my head; point to my belly, and it kind of facilitated the whole communication process." Accounting for these gestures in translation spaces is important to ensure that patients and providers understand what is being said. It also emphasizes how this part of one's linguistic repertoire connects with the embodied experience of health and illness. Rather than just talking about bodily issues in words, gesturing and using one's own body as part of the communicative process gives the patient and provider a clearer sense of the meaning of words and location of symptoms.

When explaining how he saw others communicating without words, Yoel explains that "se hacen mimica. Mimica, por ese medio" (*they mime. Miming, through that mode [they communicate]*). Similarly, Peter explains how he would act out things: "I would only know a few words so then I would try to almost act out . . . the rest of it, so even if it didn't make sense, so to speak, they had a good idea of what I was trying to ask or tell them." Because Peter worked as a dentist, he was often able to pull from a small set of vocabulary with almost every patient in addition to the physical work he did with patients' teeth. One of the cooperadoras, Miladis, also explained this process as miming, and explained how she would act out certain things when having morning conversation with participants who would visit her house for breakfast. She accompanied questions such as *How did you sleep?* (¿Cómo dormiste?) with the action of laying her head to the side on her hands to make the association with dormiste. This performance of acting out what the person wanted to say may have been a limited approach that would take a bit longer to get a point across. However, this tactic often accompanied or replaced verbal communication when faced with a loss of words or a misunderstanding.

Gestures and various forms of body language enabled individuals to fill in the blanks when they did not know a word or when their listener did not understand what they were saying. Alexis describes a moment when she was learning how to use the shower at her host family's house:

> I remember the first day, I was learning how to use my shower and some word was escaping me, so I couldn't describe any-

thing. So, basically . . . my host mom and I, we went through the whole process of how to take a shower without words because I was just too flustered to come up with the Spanish word for shower or something and I just remember feeling like such an idiot because I couldn't think of like a basic Spanish word.

Alexis describes this as an experience that she could later laugh about, but the frustration that came with forgetting specific words and not knowing alternative words to use forced her to rely on nonverbal tactics for communicating. When language learning begins with written resources, an individual may view translation as an action that is solely reliant on words. However, as many multilingual speakers can attest, when we are at a loss for words, cannot remember a word, or do not know the target language's equivalent of a word, we begin to use nonverbal tactics to get our meaning across. We point, make gestures, and move our whole bodies in ways that attempt to transmit meaning to our fellow communicator. Although we may not share common signifiers or gestures across all cultures, a deeper examination of the gestures that we do share, or of how to learn about nonverbal tactics for translanguaging, could greatly enhance our understanding of how individuals can develop their languaging potential.

Within the clinics, patients' nonverbal cues also signaled a need for the interpreter to respond or slow down the conversation in some way to minimize confusion and achieve mutual understanding. During the US participants' orientation in Santiago, there is usually a discussion of "the cultural nod." This refers to a person's gesture of nodding the head, even though she or he does not understand what the other person said. US participants noted that they saw Dominican patients doing this, and that they also did it in their own interactions with host families. Often from fear of seeming unintelligent or inconsiderate, the person enacts a cultural nod to be courteous, but the nod may express a need for further clarification. This is especially important to understand in a healthcare setting, since the doctors, dentists, and pharmacists often give instructions for the patient to follow after leaving the clinic. Jacob explains that in the clinic, interpreters needed to "make sure that every little piece of information that was really crucial was fully understood," and that "you'll have Dominicans who will say yes to you all the time in the clinic because they just don't want to be mean, or standoffish or whatever . . . but you have to make sure that they actually do understand, as opposed to just continuing with the translation." Encountering a cultural nod presents a key moment during interactions that require translation. If any possibility of misunderstanding is apparent, the interpreter needs to decide whether to continue translating, or to stop and ask whether the patient understood or if she or he could repeat back what was said. This is commonly referred to as the "teach-back method" for healthcare providers (US Dept. Health and Human Services). Additionally, in this context, the healthcare team needs to pay attention to facial expressions such as scrunching one's forehead or nose. During orientation, the healthcare team is informed that a quick scrunch or movement of a Dominican patient's nose and brow might signify "I don't understand," or "What?" This occurred daily in the clinics, and often seemed like such a natural movement that the patient might not have been consciously aware of doing it. Whether it happened midsentence or after a question, understanding the meaning of facial expressions helped the providers and interpreters know that they needed to repeat or re-articulate what they were trying to say.

The cultural nod makes it difficult to verify whether the listener actually understands, so healthcare providers and interpreters must follow up with questions about understanding and whether further clarification is needed. Elizabeth admits that misunderstanding was also common "when I was home with my [host] mom . . . because she wouldn't ever try to like rephrase things when she said them, she would just say them louder and louder and she would use the same words that I didn't know and I would just end up like saying 'Sí.' I never really knew what I was saying yes to." By acknowledging the interactions she had where meaningful conversation was lost through the façade of understanding, Elizabeth demonstrates how she enacted nonverbal gestures that patients might also use in the clinics. Additionally, her description of her host mother's language use demonstrates how the US participants experienced what many second language learners experience: people speaking louder, but not slower or in different words. These experiences can help individuals recognize the need for alternate phrasing when they speak with others, especially when there are differences in their linguistic repertoires. US participants mentioned multiple situations when Dominican patients and when they, themselves, enacted a cultural nod. The use of the cultural nod reveals a nonverbal gesture that requires attention, especially when considering the stakes of what the person might be saying yes to without knowing it.

In this chapter, I have examined how the rhetoric of translanguaging cultivates translation spaces across modes (written-spoken, nonverbal-verbal), languages (English-Spanish, Spanish-Spanish), and discourses (provider-patient discourses of health). Written texts for medical Spanish should be examined to question what "standard language" is represented and how various patients might discuss health and illness differently. By talking about, and responding to, differences in speech and text in CSR clinics, healthcare providers began to rephrase patient intake questions in ways that reflected how their patients talked about certain conditions, such as diabetes and high blood pressure. Vocabulary lists and dictionary definitions were used in new ways through meaningful interactions as ayudantes and nursing students helped each other learn ways to say certain phrases within the clinical context. Ultimately, all of these interactions helped with the development of everyone's linguistic repertoire through collaborative social action. Woven throughout these examples are stories about how all the participants cultivated their languaging repertoires because of, and in response to, the relationships they developed. Therefore, relationship building is a crucial component to the rhetoric of translanguaging, and I explore its implications in the next chapter.

5

Contexts and Collective Resources

THE RHETORIC OF TRANSLANGUAGING REQUIRES relationship building and shared goals to be used in collaborative settings. Additionally, the contexts within which individuals interact may influence their access to these collective linguistic resources. Examining how the US participants struggled to communicate when outside of the clinics and at home with their host families led to my understanding of how their time together in shared translation spaces enhanced their translanguaging potential. The difference was not just in a clinical versus nonclinical context; rather, the group was able to successfully translanguage when members were physically near others who could help them work through language variance and misunderstanding. When individuals were at home alone with their host mother or far from one of the interpreters in the group, they struggled immensely. Just as Peter described the clinic as a context that made his languaging easier because of the limited number of topics that might be discussed, nonclinical contexts opened up endless options for topics of conversation. The development of rhetorical translanguaging thrives off contexts that encourage collective action and collaborative meaning making.

People are able to translanguage together when they have overlap in their idiolects to share and make meaning together. Otheguy, García, and Reid explain,

> While no two idiolects are exactly the same lexically or structurally, there are, to be sure, large areas of overlap among the idiolects of people who communicate with each other. That is, we all share thousands of linguistic features with people

with whom we interact a lot, such as family and friends, and with people who live in the same place as we do, or who live in countries that share a history with ours, or who more generally share some sort of linguistically mediated cultural or historical identity with us. Correspondingly, we do not share many lexical or structural features with people with whom we interact less, or whose history is separate from ours. (290–91)

Based on this premise, it is not surprising that a group of students and professionals who are visiting the Dominican Republic for the first time do not comprehend the local dialect of Spanish as well as they imagined they would. However, intentionally spending time together to build relationships can lead to the development of understanding about the various lexical and structural features that differ between the ways that the local community and visiting healthcare providers communicate. This would lead to the hypothesis that the longer individuals spend together and the more intimately they share and understand each other's history and daily interactions, the more idiolectal features they might share. Even though this perspective makes one month seem like a short period of time for these participants to engage in this program together, there were interesting developments even in that short period of time that further support the role of relationship building in the rhetoric of translanguaging.

As the visiting healthcare providers encountered the complexity of language varieties and cultural differences in this program, they began to collectively develop new rhetorical strategies that were integral to the care they would deliver. This collective action centered on healthcare was driven forward because of two foundational concepts: relationship building and shared goals. With these foundations, both Dominican and visiting volunteers were able to develop their translanguaging abilities, rapport with patients, and friendships with each other.

FOSTERING CONNECTIONS

To encourage relationship building, certain structural components of the program needed to be set up to support this action and allow space for fostering connections between individuals. Clinics ran from approximately 8:00 a.m. until 1:00 p.m., Monday through Friday, for four weeks. Afternoons were set aside for relaxation and spending time at home with the community members, and all meals were eaten together at either the cooperador/a's house or one of the cocinera's (*cook's*) houses. The local community leaders worked with my assistant coordinator and me to plan evening activities. Maria, a young woman who served as a cocinera and an ayudante with groups in Buena Vista, explains how our day was organized: "En la mañana trabajamos y en la tarde siempre no(s) podemo(s) compartir todo(s) junto(s) dominicano(s) y americano(s). . . . Jugamos mucho y siempre vamos a los rio(s). Que muy divertido . . . cocinamo(s) junto(s); comimo(s) junto(s)." (*In the morning we worked and in the afternoon we always could all share time together Dominicans and Americans. . . . We played a lot and always went to the rivers. It was very fun . . . we cooked together; ate together.*) By bringing the local residents together with their visitors to go swimming, play games, cook together, and dance together, we dedicated time to foster connections across differences. These communal activities were essential to helping the group feel united and understand their time together to be something more than just work in a clinic. Also, in this way, the people we lived with were not just patients in need of a diagnosis, but also host families, neighbors, and friends. The ayudantes we worked with were more than just helpers and were truly integral companions and friends.

Although holding clinic hours for the entire day would have seemed to better "help" the community by seeing more patients, the program administrators saw value in building relationships with local residents. This also allowed the healthcare providers to rest and recharge amid the tiring process of running a clinic while adjusting to a new climate, culture, and language. Each of the visiting participants lived with a host family in the community, and many of them developed a familial-type identity with the members of those households. Many host families began calling their guests hija or hijo (*daughter* or *son*) and hermana or hermano (*sister* or *brother*), and quite a few of the visiting participants reciprocated by calling their hosts family, mom or dad, and sisters and brothers depending on the composition of the household. Not all individuals developed such an intimate relationship with their hosts, but those who did, did so regardless of their proficiency in Spanish. As a whole, the four weeks of immersion provided a constant movement of language and relationship building that enhanced the performance of the healthcare clinic and developed connections with patients and local residents.

The purpose of this program was not predominantly for language development. Language acquisition was seen as a side "perk" or possible benefit of spending time together for four weeks. However, conversational skills in Spanish or English were important for working together and bonding as a community. By building their proficiencies in various forms of English and Spanish, certain individuals were able to move back and forth between languages more easily. When discussing the Dominican ayudantes who helped in the medical clinic, Paul explains that

> they made it very interesting to interact in the clinical setting because we couldn't always just revert to English. . . . Over the course of the four weeks that we worked with them, I did notice that we obviously grew more comfortable with them and . . . I think they, without a doubt, grew more comfortable with us, and that was a very fruitful relationship and one that ended up being very beneficial for us in the clinical setting.

These relationships did enhance the clinical interactions and the languaging development for all members of the healthcare team. Both the need to challenge themselves to speak in Spanish while running the clinic and the ways participants grew more comfortable with each other developed a rhetorical familiarity (Guerra) that was important to the collaboration that could happen in the clinic.

García and Wei state, "Translanguaging refers to the flexibility of bilingual learners to take control of their own learning, to self-regulate when and how to language, depending on the context in which they're being asked to perform" (80). I noticed both Dominican and US participants taking up this control of their own learning in a variety of contexts, which contributed to their ability to retain and incorporate their new linguistic and cultural knowledge. In my field notes on July 10, 2012, I wrote,

> The team has been good at asking how to say things in Spanish and trying to say them instead of just relying on one of us to translate.
> -dinner—asking for a fork, spoon, water, etc. in the kitchen
> -clinic—have a good day, you're going to feel a few pinches but after, you won't feel pain, lots of pressure but no pain, and other dental/pharmacy instructions.

To explain further, the US participants might turn to me or another team member and ask, "How do I ask for a fork?" Then, after hearing the phrase and repeating it a few times, they would go to the kitchen and articulate their question to the cocinera. This short note resonated with interview data about how a number of the visiting team members tried to take control of their learning and enable themselves to translanguage in moments when an interpreter was not present. Since full fluency was not possible to acquire in just four weeks, participants focused on short phrases and words that they could learn and then use when connecting with each other.

Our group dynamic enhanced this move to self-regulate when and how to language. Nicole notes that there were various team members who could help with her language-learning process while working in the clinic. She explains that what helped her with "translating" (but what I saw as translanguaging) was "asking whoever's helping, whoever was translating for us; the coordinator, the assistant coordinator, just random people in the back [of the clinic], having them repeat it three or four times for me, and saying it myself." The way that Nicole transformed moments of translation into opportunities for learning was a self-empowering move. By taking the initiative to ask for repetition and then to re-articulate words herself, Nicole used the group's linguistic resources to develop her Spanish languaging repertoire.

I often told the youth of the towns, and the US participants, that the local residents were some of my best Spanish teachers. Whenever a local resident would help me better understand a new phrase, I would thank him or her by saying Gracias, profe (*Thank you, prof[essor]*). The deeply engrained relationship of acting as language teachers in our interactions was also apparent during my interviews with Dominican participants. When describing a phrase in English that he had learned, Miguel says this:

> MIGUEL: Never give up [pronounced "oop"] . . . como nunca te rinda en inglés (. . . *like never give up in English.*)
> RAQUEL: Cuál es? (*Which is?*) [I did not understand it the first time he said it.]
> MIGUEL: Never . . . give up.
> RAQUEL: Nunca . . . te rinda?
> MIGUEL: Rinda, rinda, rendirse.

By repeating the word and conjugating it for me, I was able to catch what Miguel said and learn a new term that I was not familiar with before the interview. As he told me about a phrase he had learned in English, Miguel actually taught me a new phrase in Spanish.

Katy also explains that the Dominicans who wanted to connect with their visitors across language difference should preguntarle, "Yo quiero aprender inglés. . . . ¿Qué significa esto? ¿Qué significa aquello?" (*Ask them, "I want to learn English. . . . What does this mean? What does that mean?"*) Taking that step to ask for help in learning the meaning of words and their pronunciations was one that both Dominican and US participants saw as beneficial. By drawing from the collective resources of the group, individuals could enable themselves to move toward more self-sufficiency in connecting with others across linguistic difference. Daniel adds that when he heard others speak English, "Mi experiencia era que cada palabra que decían, yo lo entendía un poco. Entonce(s), cuando no entendía algunas, le preguntaba y así aprendía más." (*My experience was that each word that they said, I understood a little. Then, when I did not understand some [words], I asked and in this way I learned more.*) Just as Daniel emphasizes that he would ask questions about the meaning of words when he did not understand them, other participants mention the need to slow people down or ask for clarification in order to learn and acquire new words and phrases.

All of the Dominican ayudantes that I interviewed described their interest in learning English in relation to the benefits that came with time spent with the US participants. Katy was preparing to begin classes at the local university for teaching English and French at the time of our interview, and she explains, "Me interesa mucho aprender inglés e involucrándome con demás personas que estén hablando ese idioma como que me ayudaba desarrollarme aprender más, entender más en inglés, o sea, escuchar otro hablándolo. Me ayudó muchísimo en lo que es y va a ser mi vida profesional de hoy y adelante." (*I'm very interested in learning English and getting involved with other people who speak this language in the ways that it helps me learn more, understand more in English, that is, to listen to another person speaking it. It helped me so much with what my professional life is today and what it will be in the future.*) For Katy, learning and practicing English with the visitors was not only beneficial for her work in this program but also for her future studies and career. Additionally, Miguel explains how these intercultural interactions instilled a desire to learn English, and that the time together was "una experiencia inolvidable que, a veces quería saber lo que estaban diciendo y no podía . . . no(s) motivo mucha(s) persona(s) saber inglés para otro grupo un día saber lo que estaban diciendo" (*an unforgettable experience that, at times, I wanted to know what they were saying and I was not able to . . . it motivates a lot of us to learn English for another group one day to understand what they were saying*). Since Buena Vista had hosted the summer program the year before I worked there, Miguel knew that there was a possibility that another group would return in the future. Even though CSR switches communities every two to three years with this program, the local residents expressed hope for hosting another group in the near future. This provided an incentive for learning English outside of the program to prepare for future interactions with English speakers who might visit and live with the community. Although many of the young residents had taken English classes in school, they explained that it was not the same as having conversations with their visitors in this program. Both local residents and visiting participants noted this special component of building both relationships and linguistic repertoires together, which proved to complement and build on their classroom learning of languaging.

Although success in translanguaging varied by participant, even just observing others in the group helped with comprehension. This observation might include listening to interpreters and patients having dialogues or watching bilingual participants translanguage. Abby states, "I don't think that I picked up more that I was able to speak, but I got to the point where I could understand more . . . which was very helpful 'cause even though I couldn't communicate back to them, at least I was able to listen." Noting this ability to gain understanding before the ability to articulate and speak fluently was a common observation from US participants who had basic to intermediate proficiency in Spanish. However, in my observations, I did notice that this process was a bit more complicated and fluid than these participants thought it was. Although they may not have held fluent conversations or known how to conjugate words, participants like Abby did language in Spanish. What prevented their "ability" to communicate in Spanish was most likely more a question of confidence, practice, and confirmation rather than the comprehension of the meaning of words and how they are pronounced. Five of the US interviewees mentioned that they felt they could understand Spanish more than they could speak. This may have been influenced by the way I phrased the question: "What languages do you know how to speak and understand?" What would have been helpful to further investigate this point would be to consider what factors influenced an individual's confidence in pronouncing words, articulating points, and connecting sentences rather than a general question about what she or he "understood" or "could speak." What can be drawn from this data is that translanguaging can account for different stages of language development, and translingual research should interrogate those stages as an important part of the process of developing rhetorical adaptability in multilingual settings.

Further drawing on the value of listening to others when they are speaking, Nicole mentions how the unique nature of their cross-cultural group helped with her language development. She explains, "When an American and a Dominican were talking, the Dominicans tend to slow their speech a little bit and the Americans definitely have slower Spanish, and to see the facial interactions and everything like that, I was able to somewhat understand a word or two." This example of listening to conversations demonstrates how this situated context set up certain conditions that made it easier for participants with basic proficiency in the language to learn new words and phrases. By spending time with both US and Dominican participants and hearing how both of them had slower speech habits together, Nicole was able to recognize situations in which she could try to follow along and learn. The process of acquiring new words and phrases in Spanish allowed Nicole to develop new connections with individuals she could not communicate with at the beginning of the program. As various members of this healthcare team helped each other develop new language skills, they developed their linguistic repertoires in ways that enhanced the care they could provide to the community.

The various stages of language development and the process of shuttling across languages represent a constant negotiation of translanguaging in this collective. As Horner, NeCamp, and Donahue state,

> Rather than striving for "fluency in" a particular language or set of languages, we believe it more appropriate, and more broadly accessible, to develop ways to grow fluent in working across and among languages. . . . While the ambition of achieving a high degree of fluency in another language is certainly admirable, its pursuit can prevent the flexible, fluid relationship with languages we believe might be more effective for this work. (287–88)

This flexible, fluid relationship with languages can lessen the pressure of being able to perform language "perfectly," and instead focuses on the ways we grow fluent in developing our rhetorical sensibilities across languages. In addition, the development of language learning within informal contexts and authentic conversations as they happen in practice can better prepare individuals for the challenges of professional work across languages. The participants in this study who were able to take a more flexible approach to language learning were more easily able to develop their rhetorical sensibilities in working across languages and, in turn, develop connections with patients and local volunteers.

TRANSLANGUAGING TO CONNECT

Katy explains that she saw a change in the local community as they began to try out new phrases in English during the four weeks when the participants lived together: "Los niños . . . decían palabras en inglés que ya yo aprendía un poco y le escuchaban, 'Ah, hello! Good morning!' Se ha saludaban a los americanos. . . . Entonce(s) allí no(s) mezclábamos y podíamos trabajar todo satisfactoriamente." (*The children . . . they said words in English that I had already learned a little and they heard, 'Ah, hello! Good morning!' They greeted the Americans. . . . So there we mixed together and were able to work with everything successfully.*) In observing how the children began using English greetings, Katy saw interest in language learning as something that helped set up conditions for a good mezcla (*mixture*) between cultures. Simple phrases such as those used in greeting each other every day were small steps that the children, or anyone, could take to make positive connections with each other. Similarly, many of the US participants began greeting their host families and neighbors each morning with ¡Hola! ¡Buenos días! (*Hello! Good morning!*) Taking advantage of these moments of morning saludos (*greetings*) and using each other's linguistic resources contributed to this collective's connections outside of the clinic. The local residents saw these translingual moves as ways to make their visitors feel welcome, and the visiting participants saw them as opportunities to engage the community in personally meaningful ways.

Additionally, for the US participants, incorporating regional terminology of the community's Spanish dialect demonstrated that one "knew" the language and could connect with local residents. Paul recounts,

> I found that when I was able to incorporate the phrases, or colloquialisms, of that region or of the DR, the people often lit up or were excited about somebody knowing about their idiosyncrasy of that language. So, even if I were to say it in a joking manner . . . I'm confiding in you that I'm speaking in your language, I'm saying "Hey look, pin-pun, they look the same," or . . . "it's just 'un chin' of this," or a little of that, then they often responded very kindly to that and seemed to appreciate that I was making an extra effort.

Paul's description articulates how the rhetorical strategies of incorporating Dominicanisms into one's Spanish languaging helped with connecting across differences. Although team members must be careful that in an attempt to make others laugh, they are not mocking the Spanish of the community, finding ways to demonstrate an understanding of Dominicanisms seemed to be received well. The visiting participants were able to develop personally meaningful connections by recognizing phrases and terms that were valued in the community discourse. Doing so also developed their ethos as knowing how to speak Spanish in this specific context, which valued the rural Dominican Spanish of the region.

In their interviews, both Dominican and US participants shared stories about how they supported each other's translanguaging with fun phrases unique to each other's community and culture. These stories speak to the relationship building that developed beyond the clinical context. One example of bonding over playful language occurred in Buena Vista, when local residents were singing a song that they thought the US participants would immediately recognize. Miguel says that he and his friends realized they had it all wrong "con una canción de una vez que aquí decíamos [laughs] 'Sha-ke-ton' y decía Jacobo no, que era 'Who let the dogs out?'" (*with a song one time that here we said "Sha-ke-ton" and Jacob said that no, it was*

"Who let the dogs out?"). He adds, "Estuvimos todo el día riendo. No conocimos . . ." (*We were laughing all day. We didn't know [that we were singing the wrong words]*). What Miguel was referring to were the lyrics that he and others were singing, "Who let the dogs out?" as "un-sha-ke-ton-ton" from the popular song by Baha Men released in 2000. After Jacob explained the lyrics in English and translated them into Spanish, the local residents found it extremely comical that they had been singing what sounded like the words without knowing their actual meaning in the song. Although it may appear to be an insignificant interaction when looking at relations among participants in a temporary healthcare program, a moment like this represented some of the most memorable interactions for participants. Not only were these moments memorable in showing how participants enjoyed time together, but they were also significant in how individuals learned new ways to translanguage because of their time together.

Playing and communicating with children in the town also helped visitors who had less proficiency in Spanish interact with the community. Whether they decided to draw together or play with toys, visitors found that nonverbal communication had a lot of potential for making connections with children in the community. Abby shares that one of "the kids at my host family's house—we would draw pictures in the dirt, and then she would use Spanish to explain it, but then she would also take her stick and point out things and draw things for me." Abby added that the girls would become frustrated at times when she did not understand what they were saying, but that this use of drawing and pointing was one approach for remedying a language barrier in order to spend time together. Similarly, Nicole had an experience when she took shelter from the rain at a nearby house and began playing with a boy, Marco, who lived there. She explains that he had a toy alligator, and they

> kinda just got this little bond going and playing. . . . The sounds that I was making of "Chomp, chomp, chomp, chomp, chomp!" . . . repeating the sound and doing the actions, he would start to repeat them to me. So I knew we were

somewhat communicating of this is the action. . . . I would take one of my fingers and roll it over and he would understand that I thought that meant he just ate my finger and so when I did it to him, he would do the same. . . . I don't think during that entire playing time a single actual word was said.

Nicole's experience illuminates the importance of play, repetition, and the use of material objects for communicating beyond traditional notions of languaging with words. The one "word" that was said in their interaction represented a sound Nicole was trying to make to signify the biting action of the alligator. My sense is that there was also laughter and other sounds made in their time playing together. In this form of translanguaging, Marco listened and received the message Nicole was making and, in turn, reciprocated with the same message to signal that he enjoyed that way of playing with his toy alligator. Whether the children were trying to teach their visitors new words by drawing or they just wanted to enjoy time playing together, they showed the US participants that it was possible to make connections even with limited overlap in idiolects.

Nonverbal communication could provide space for making connections across differences when individuals were faced with a loss of words or wanted to accompany words with meaningful gestures. Jacob describes how people can connect in various nonverbal ways: "the smiles that people have, the kind of quirky humors or whatever, just like playing pranks on people, or walking up and giving someone a good handshake or a kiss on the cheek." However, he adds, "I think that verbal communication is more meaningful in terms of forming deeper relationships. . . . I mean you can only do so much on a nonverbal level." This was a common perception for participants with more advanced proficiency in Spanish, including myself. I was intrigued with the connections participants could make without having much Spanish proficiency, but I began this study with a bias that having more advanced proficiency would result in deeper connections. Not until holding these interviews and following up with community members in the years after the program did I realize that the ways participants and local residents had connected were simply different depending on a variety of factors.

Not only did local residents ask about their guests from previous programs years after, but the host families who would also spend my entire follow-up visit talking about their American *hijo* or *hija* were most often those who had hosted US participants who spoke the least amount of Spanish.

In addition to the verbal phrases that they learned, participants also taught each other nonverbal ways to make connections, and demonstrated an ability to show care through their actions. In a follow-up meeting two years after we worked together, I asked Miladis whether it was possible to have a connection with patients even without the language or with an interpreter. She said yes, "porque el amor de ustedes . . . " (*because your love . . .*), and I asked, "¿Se mostraron en otras maneras?" (*They showed in other ways?*) She replied, "Exactamente." (*Exactly.*) Following this, Miladis began to recount the story about a day when Nicole had an exceptionally difficult dental procedure. What was expected to be a twenty-minute appointment turned into a four-hour-long process filled with vomiting, nausea, tears, prayers, and a communal effort to support our young dentist working to extract a wisdom tooth without any of the x-rays or equipment she would have had back in the United States. In what Miladis described as a day she would never forget with tanto amor (*so much love*), Nicole and her patient made it through a physically and emotionally tiring process in which Nicole did not speak much Spanish and the patient spoke only a few words amid the pain and nausea he felt during the procedure.

Nicole describes this procedure as "an emotional experience," and states that even though she felt an overwhelming amount of relief and joy once she finally had extracted the tooth completely, she also worried about how the patient would heal and hoped she could follow up with him after the procedure: "I hope I just know you're okay tomorrow and I hope everything goes okay tonight and you're able to sleep. . . . It's now a bond him and I have that is something that I probably will never have with another person because we together—I'm sure he was going through those same emotions—went together through them, and this . . . this sense of connection between him and I." Because she felt (and demonstrated in her actions) empathy for his pain and wanted to be sure that he recovered well, Nicole was able to make a connection with this patient despite her limited proficiency in Spanish. Years later, Miladis, the patient, and the patient's father still mention that as an incredibly moving experience in which they saw how much the visiting team cared about the patients of the local community. The father also mentioned that it was additionally meaningful to see me care so much for his son. This was probably one of the most stressful days of the two summers I worked with these teams. Toward the end of the procedure, I realized that there was nothing I could do except to keep checking in to translate, sit, and watch. I began to pray because I had no idea what else to do, and when Nicole finally pulled the tooth out, I had to step away because I was immediately overcome with tears. We demonstrate so much through our actions and embodied languaging. As members of a healthcare team, it is important to recognize that patients are not the only ones whose bodies are "read" in patient-provider interactions.

As I mentioned in Chapter 4, the dental clinic was an interesting site for studying nonverbal communication, and because of that, the relationships that providers seemed to develop with patients were admired by others in the group. The dental students in Rancho de la Vaca were noted as having an exceptional ability to connect with patients despite their limited Spanish proficiency. Elizabeth explains that with

> Peter, our dental student, who spoke like zero Spanish, I felt sometimes that people understood him better than they understood me. Even with his poorly pronounced, one- [and] two-word Spanish, just like his facial expressions and his pointing, I don't know, people . . . they understood him, which was amazing to me because, even though I could put a sentence together, I still felt like people just looked at me like they had no clue what I was saying.

Multiple participants mentioned Peter's ability to connect with patients and local residents without being proficient in Spanish. His humor and ability to use gestures creatively with simple Spanish words was something that put patients at ease in the dental area, made all team members laugh during tense situations, and impressed the volunteers at the clinic. One example is how he asked almost every patient if they liked his bigote (*mustache*), which he had grown out during his time there. He had first asked me how to phrase the question, and then repeated it a few times before trying it out with a new patient. Smiling and raising his eyebrows as he pointed to his mustache, Peter constantly infused laughter into the atmosphere of the dental clinic. Peter's lighthearted approach to translanguaging enabled him to forge connections despite his limited Spanish proficiency. Alexis explains that "some of the coolest connections that are made are [with] the people who come down and they don't really know much Spanish, and they really stretch themselves to practice their Spanish, especially with their host family. I thought Peter did a great job . . . jumping into the culture and trying to get everything he could out of the experience." She added that Peter and Joshua would try to talk with their host family every night despite multiple moments of misunderstanding and translation errors. This willingness to engage in translanguaging, even at a what seemed like a basic level with a large portion of nonverbal gestures, was motivated by the desire to develop emotional connections with people in and outside of the clinic.

The nonverbal connections that individuals made reflected local gestures and values, and ultimately contributed to the group's ability to connect across differences. The US participants also learned that sitting with others could be an important action to take in being present with their host families. Paul explains,

> One of the major lessons I learned in the Dominican Republic . . . was the value of sitting. I came to appreciation of how much, especially in their culture, but now that I've contemplated it further, in our own, we value when people sit with us. In the Dominican Republic, if you don't sit down when you visit somebody it really wasn't a visit. . . . The first thing that the majority of the people would say when we'd either walk through their threshold or near their home was, "Sit down, sit down, have a seat."

Paul and other participants also mentioned how surprised they were by how quickly local residents could round up a large number of plastic chairs to have everyone in the visiting group sit together on someone's front porch. The host often proceeded to offer coffee or food, demonstrating a constant reminder of the hospitality of the local residents.

The US participants recognized this value of spending time with others, and even sitting in silence together, as a cultural way of connecting that they felt seemed to be lost in their own fast-paced culture at home. In my field notes from July 1, 2012, I wrote about a moment when Miladis made me aware of my own embodiment of this fast-paced culture:

> I [was] having un cafecito antes de la misa (*a coffee before mass*) enjoying a calm, cool morning here in [Rancho de la Vaca]. After I poured my coffee and mixed the sugar, I started sipping it while I was still standing. Miladis told me a saying they have here that says, "Si tomas café a pie, van a bajar todo de tus planes para el dia." (*If you drink your coffee while standing, all of your plans for the day will fall apart.*) She explained how you need to take the time to sit and enjoy your coffee so not to rush through everything else.

After sitting and enjoying my coffee, I rushed to write this down to add to the list of things that Miladis taught me about cultural ways of communicating and experiencing the world. (Yes, I realize the irony in this statement, but it's what I did, further demonstrating the cultural dissonance of this moment.) Miladis explained that not only was sitting important for spending time with other people, but also community members felt it was important for one's personal health and outlook on the day.

By sitting with people, and compartiendo juntos (*sharing [time] together*) outside of the clinic, the US participants opened themselves to new relationships. When they were sitting on a neighbor's porch, sipping a freshly brewed taza de café (*cup of coffee*), and listening to conversations about the weather, they set aside their role as healthcare provider and took up the identity of companion and guest. The relationships that developed in these liminal times, between patient visits, clinic hours, and planned activities, made the translanguaging and healthcare possible and more seamless with each day we spent together. Taking the time to nurture these relationships and learn from small instances of community discourse—whether it was terminology used when playing games of dominoes or gestures to demonstrate care and hospitality—allowed the visitors to gain new insights into language and culture. Developing these relationships further demonstrated the care that the visiting team members had for their patients through their efforts to better understand their patients' daily lives and discourse. This, in turn, solidified their commitment to learning from, and working with, the local community in running these temporary clinics.

MISSED CONNECTIONS

The context of individuals' interactions and their access to others in the group greatly influenced their positive and negative reactions to instances of translanguaging. Being together in the same physical space allowed participants to share linguistic resources. Although the majority of participants felt that connections across differences and collaboration were possible, this was not the case for everyone. When individuals attempted to translanguage, it sometimes resulted in unpredictable, negative interactions. Additionally, certain factors may have influenced some participants negatively in ways that dissuaded them from wanting to try translanguaging.

For the local residents, having little to no proficiency in English may have affected their willingness to interact with, or say anything to, US participants when they were speaking in English. When I asked what her experience was like hearing others speak in English around her, one of the cooperadoras de salud, Rosa, explained, "La experiencia e(s) que como yo no entiendo me quedo callada. Pero, despué(s) quizá(s) si me interesa yo le pregunto a uno que sepa, especialmente a la supervisor(a), para que me diga que fue lo que ello(s) dijero(n) . . . para saber." (*The experience is that since I do not understand [English] I stay silent. But, after, perhaps if I'm interested I will ask someone who knows, especially the supervisor, to tell me what it was that they said . . . to understand.*) When Rosa did not ask me or another participant to translate, she was left out of the conversation and remained quiet because of her exclusion. Even Dominican participants with basic or moderate proficiency in English had trouble following conversations that the US participants had in English. Therefore, many Dominicans were excluded when the group turned to English-only conversations without offering interpretation in Spanish.

There were also times when the US participants felt left out of conversations. In my analysis, the persistent mention of moments when US participants felt like an "outsider," "othered" in some way, or "foreign" made this a theme worth noting as part of the negative aspects that may have led to an aversion to translanguaging. The most common instance of this came in US participants' description of worrying about, or not knowing whether, someone was talking about them. Elizabeth explains,

> I'm going to a Spanish-speaking country . . . it wasn't like I thought people would magically speak English there. I mean it's hard because it's like well, I have no idea, they could be talking about me, and I have no idea what they're saying. Like they could be saying I'm a complete idiot because I don't speak Spanish, which you know, they might have been, because sometimes I'm sure I sounded like an idiot when I tried to say things.

Saying she sounded like an idiot was similar to negative terms that other participants used to describe how they might be perceived by others. Nicole shares a similar sentiment when explaining about a time when her host mother was trying to ask her a question: "I found out later she was asking where our towels were . . . but all I could catch was 'towel was hanging there' and I was like, 'Yeah, that's my towel,' and didn't really get that she was asking me. . . . But I did say 'That's my towel!' and she just looked at me like I was insane." I aided in Nicole's follow-up conversation, when she asked me to interpret and figure out what her host mom had been saying to her. That visit demonstrated her use of our collective resources in response to disconnect with her first experience with the conversation and my ability to comprehend her host mother's languaging more completely. More than likely, these interactions and their hosts' perceptions were probably not as extreme as the US participants imagined, but it is important to note when participants felt foreign, and like an "other" who was unable to communicate. These moments allow students who have never experienced the feeling of being "othered" as a linguistic and cultural minority to understand the frustrations and complexities that come with translanguaging in a new environment and being separated from the collective linguistic resources of the group.

Jackie had similar experiences of disconnect with her host family and did not really feel that a deep relationship was ever developed. However, she noted that this experience of "seeing a new culture, being immersed in it, it gave me a lot of empathy towards immigrants who are coming here [to the United States], 'cause I didn't understand that, you know, not being able to speak the language is . . . just very frustrating." Although these feelings of frustration may not have subsided during the program for Jackie, she did see a way in which understanding that experience of not being able to communicate in a new language and culture could be transferred to experiences back home. This demonstrates the importance of having an individual experience frustration through taking risks in translanguaging. If translanguaging seeks to make more just social structures, then part of that structural change can begin with empathy for others.

Even when US participants tried to incorporate tactics for communicating, like using dictionaries, some of them still ran into moments when they could not make a connection. Joshua explains, "It's kind of a double-edged sword because it felt like sometimes like when we were trying to talk to our mom and dad . . . I mean we had gotten our Spanish dictionary out and we were workin' hard just to say something to her and we couldn't get it across. I felt like it was kind of like they're not talking behind your back . . . it's like talking about you to your face, but you can't understand." By invoking language similar to Elizabeth's—others talking about you but not knowing what they've said—Joshua described what was clearly a frustrating experience. These experiences, especially when at their hosts' houses, represented moments of being isolated from their collective resources and interpreters at the clinics. Participants who could help ease the negotiation of languages and interpretation were not always readily available, and therefore, individuals might have lost motivation to keep struggling through language difference when they could not comprehend words in the process.

Joshua and a couple of the other participants also encountered issues that reflected the class differences and potential struggles that come with integrating participants from privileged and marginalized communities. In the CSR guidebook, a specific section on ways to give back to the community is included under the heading "Donations," which states,

> Do NOT give gifts or donations to your host family or friends in the campo. It is extremely important to not set a precedent of gift-giving. Th[is] will cause an uncomfortable situation for future CSR participants who could serve in the same community. If you want to donate money or clothing for your campo, please bring it to the CSR Center's front office before you leave. (El Centro para la Salud Rural 38)

For some participants, this was a difficult rule to abide by since they had developed strong emotional connections with their host families. However, the program administrators were right that these actions could lead to future interactions that might be uncomfortable for visitors and host communities. A couple of individuals encountered difficult situations when their host families asked them to leave a belonging behind when returning to the United States. Joshua explains that the situation felt worse because he did not understand what was being said, and had to prolong the interaction by getting someone to come and interpret for him. He explains that his and Peter's host dad

> kept pointing to our watch and I thought that he was saying that, like "at this time tomorrow, I'll be gone" or something. And we're like oh, you know we'll miss you, and we'll have

Charlie come over later and translate tonight so we can have our proper goodbye. And it turns out he actually wanted our watch when he left . . . which is I'm sure why we don't give gifts or whatever. . . . I wasn't really offended too much either way. But it was like, this sucks that I can't understand.

Peter and Joshua did not give the watch as a present, but this interaction brings up various issues that can arise when (1) individuals from very different class backgrounds spend time together in the setting of a service program, and when (2) a participant is placed in a difficult ethical situation but does not know how to articulate, or understand completely, what is being discussed. A similar instance happened with another US participant (not interviewed) when the host father in Buena Vista asked for his tennis shoes. Although these scenarios are often remedied by having respectful conversations with the coordinators and cooperadores, homestays may add another dimension to the complicated relations that can arise in transnational and transcultural community-engaged programs.

COLLABORATION

For the majority of my participants, collective actions made translanguaging possible, and drawing on each other's resources helped individuals form personal connections. Developing comfort with other members of the temporary collective, camaraderie when stressful situations happened, and a sense of unity as a team running the clinic on a daily basis resulted in an overall positive experience. Alexis explains that during the program, she saw "a really cool kind of collaboration between the Dominicans and the Americans," especially in the ways "that the Dominicans are so excited that we're trying to learn Spanish and you know if we screw up . . . they're very patient with us, so I think that's one neat connection that's made is bonding over the language barrier." Similarly, when I asked Katy to discuss the relationships among participants from different backgrounds, she said they were excellent, explaining,

> Por ejemplo, la cultura de nosotros, Dominicano y Americano, trabajar con ellos fue muy satisfactorio porque mucho(s)

hablaban español; sabían bien español. Algunos aquí interpretábamos algo de inglés y no(s) mezclamos juntos y cada cual aprendió de la cultura diferente. Aprendimos de lo(s) americano(s) y ello(s) de lo(s) dominicano(s). (*For example, our culture, Dominican and American, to work with them was very rewarding because many of them spoke Spanish; they knew Spanish well. Some people here, we interpreted something from English and we mixed together and each one learned from the different culture. We learned from the Americans and they [learned] from the Dominicans.*)

Learning from each other's culture and language use aided the development of relationships within the program and supported the work carried out in the clinics. By mezclando (*mixing*) across differences, these participants found the motivation to negotiate languages and take risks with communication in order to more effectively work and enjoy their time together.

Collaboration across differences was possible because of a unifying purpose: to serve the healthcare needs of the local community and sustain these clinics for four weeks. The contexts in which participants communicated also enabled their translanguaging confidence and abilities. Joshua explains,

I think it's maybe easier to kind of communicate from different cultures when you have a purpose that unifies you . . . we were there for the same reason, for the same purpose every day . . . [and] I think when you're there for other people, I think you're going to be more open to communicating with someone that's not from your culture because it's not about you; it's about the person you're helping.

Joshua's description of what unified the US and Dominican volunteers in the clinics highlights what drove him and others to persevere through struggles with translanguaging. Peter echoes the description of a common goal, and explains that in the dental clinic, they would "communicate through a common goal of tryin' to address some kind of oral health need that [the patients] have." The context of clinical settings shaped how individuals translanguaged together; in turn, the relationships that they built helped accomplish their shared goals within this context: to care for the patients and keep the clinic running each day.

If translanguaging is transdisciplinary, then temporary healthcare programs like CSR's provide an interesting site for studying how professionals communicate across various disciplines in healthcare. Among the US participants, individuals noted that there was collaboration across differences based on their regional "homes" in the United States and their various disciplinary backgrounds. Joshua liked how the CSR program allowed "all the professions to come together, because you don't see that. Well, just not as much—you'll rarely see a dentist and a physician interact, you know?" This was a similar response across most of the US interviewees when I asked about "people from different backgrounds coming together." I originally wrote that interview question with an assumption that the responses would focus on working with someone from a different nation or language, but many US participants discussed working with other US participants since most of them did not know each other prior to the trip, and they came from various regions and medical specialties. The program provided a unique clinical setting that featured much cross-cultural communication, but it also required daily collaboration across health profession roles (doctors, dentists, pharmacists, nurses, and undergraduate helpers).

The US participants' collaboration across differences increased with their bonds over the immersion experience of this program. Matthew explains,

> I think it was easy for us to come together in the group because we all are facing these new challenges together, so everybody kind of understands what everyone's going through, and you can have a laugh about a giant spider in your bathroom, or you can have someone understand your frustration when you're trying to communicate with the patients and they look at you like you have three heads.

These new challenges came in many forms, and Matthew's summary from the spider to miscommunication demonstrates the variety of new experiences participants encountered in the four weeks they were in the campo. Matthew's description of a shared experience of having patients "look at you like you have three heads" is also important to note. His descriptive simile refers to the moments of experiencing a language barrier, and the nonverbal cues of misunderstanding shown by patients in the clinics. This resonates with Elizabeth's and Nicole's descriptions of worrying that people thought they "sounded like an idiot" or were "insane." To cope with these feelings of "otherness," the US participants bonded over shared dilemmas with language differences.

When used productively, the connections developed through a shared struggle with translanguaging led to the collective language learning and rhetorical adaptability of the healthcare team. Individuals would not have pursued translanguaging if they thought they were the only ones experiencing problems of feeling foreign or like an outsider. Also, without the recognition of translanguaging as a communal activity, there may not have been as many instances of participants cultivating translation spaces across verbal, nonverbal, written, and oral forms. With each attempt at negotiating languages, dialects, and gestures, participants discovered new ways to communicate and connect with the varied members of this collective: volunteers, community leaders, patients, and host families.

Before concluding this chapter, I want to acknowledge the materiality of this experience and how it might also have influenced individuals' willingness to translanguage. As Grabill argues, "Rhetoric is always material, and it is most powerful when it makes things that enable others to perform persuasively" ("On Being" 201). Although some aspects of this program enabled a more flexible and fluid approach to translanguaging, other material components may have left individuals tired, uncomfortable, or unable to feel positive about translanguaging from their full linguistic repertoires. For the local community members, it was uncomfortable and challenging to welcome strangers from a different culture into their homes for four weeks. They faced challenges in caring for the visitors, many of whom did not speak their language, did not know how to shower or do any daily tasks in the same ways as the local residents, and needed constant help and guidance or clarification in order to communicate with each other. Additionally, the visitors represented (whether they wanted to or not) an additional pressure as representatives and guests of CSR. For communities to maintain positive relationships with administrators at CSR and to host future clinics, community members would want everything to go smoothly, and to be sure their visitors left with a positive impression of the community. This added stress and discomfort would have undoubtedly affected how often the local residents interacted with their visitors or attempted to translanguage with them.

The US participants were also adjusting to many challenges, including (but not limited to) dealing with extreme heat with no air conditioning, using latrines rather than toilets with running water, eating culturally specific food on a preset schedule, sleeping in close quarters with people they had just met, and being constantly surrounded by the sounds of farm animals and a fast-paced, unfamiliar form of Spanish. The material differences from the participants' daily lives required the ability to adapt constantly as they navigated life in the campo for four weeks. Miladis asked me many times about how the visiting group adjusted when they came from a place where "viven con todas las comodidades" (*they live with all of the comforts*) and left their families for such a long time to live in the campo, sleep with mosquiteros (*mosquito nets*), and deal with el calor (*the heat*). The physical experience of living in these towns during June and July, when most participants would have had air-conditioned offices or homes in the United States, must be accounted for in the ways that it influenced, and at times prevented, the motivation to engage in translingual negotiation and collaboration across differences. Theoretically, making connections across differences while providing healthcare is a noble and important goal. In practice, trying to achieve this goal while also dealing with increased heat, mosquito bites, indigestion, diarrhea, anxiety, and a constant battle with dehydration proves to be a bit more difficult.

Although these challenges are important to acknowledge, the context for this program also led to beneficial conditions for collective translanguaging. The unique aspect of staying with host families for four weeks is that healthcare providers are constantly surrounded by the language and culture of their patients. Whereas US medical students might volunteer at a clinic in an urban or rural neighborhood near their school, these institutional settings limit the time when participants will encounter their patients and local community discourses. The students return to their homes, and unless they share communal ties of language practices with their various patients, they will spend the majority of their days surrounded by discourses of privilege and difference in relation to what they encounter in the clinical settings. But when they work and live with local community members, especially those living in poverty, healthcare practitioners tend to learn more about who their patients are and why they come to the clinic talking about certain issues in certain ways. When healthcare practitioners share the same water filters as their patients, or notice a lack of clean water, they realize that dehydration in this intense heat might be a very real health concern, along with waterborne diseases. As Alexis explains, "A good part of the experience [is that] you really are living with the people and when you eat what they eat, and I mean . . . no wonder so many people come in with digestive problems to our clinic because of their eating" plantains, rice and beans, and other starchy foods. She also mentions "how good mangoes are for you but when you eat too many of them, with all the sugar, you know . . . they can cause dental issues, [and] help cause diabetes that we saw so many patients had." Within a context of seeing many sugary drinks, candy, and other "unhealthy" foods being eaten on a daily basis, these students and professionals learned what people ate and what was available in the region, and gradually developed better recommendations based on that understanding. This is not to say that all visiting practitioners learn about their patients and host families by living together for four weeks. Being able to fluently converse, understand the host family's language use, and feel comfortable enough to engage with them greatly influences the potential for this learning. The relationship building that happened outside of the clinics simultaneously influenced the practitioners' ability to translanguage and provide care within the clinics. Even though this study represents a unique circumstance that cannot, and should not, be replicated for everyone, the potential for developing more rhetorically adept and caring providers remains entrenched in the providers' intentional interaction with the communities they serve.

This chapter examined how relationship building is foundational to the rhetoric of translanguaging. It discussed how participants took advantage of translation spaces to develop their linguistic repertoires and connect across cultures. Both Dominican and US participants used colloquial sayings and discursive tactics to mirror one another's languaging. Alternatively, considering the risks that came with translanguaging illuminates concerns of feeling like an outsider. Moments of disconnect surface when differences in language, culture, and class further alienate individuals from making connections or wanting to engage in translanguaging. Ultimately, this chapter demonstrated how the majority of participants felt that collaboration was possible through their collective negotiations of differences and their shared purpose for serving the community together.

In their downtime between patients, participants supported each other's language development. Walking along the dirt path toward the clinic, Dominican children shouted greetings in English to their visitors. Participants bonded over humor, songs, and play. Relationships formed, and translanguaging was possible because of these relationships and the rhetorical familiarity that came with them. When Dominican and US participants saw translation spaces as opportunities for learning, individuals were empowered to make new connections with patients through future performances of certain words or phrases. Without taking risks and making mistakes, they would not have turned to each other as much or bonded across the language barrier. The temporary healthcare teams in this study were rhetorical in their use of translanguaging because of how they complicated language ideologies, transformed texts and notions of translation, and built relationships across differences to further develop their translanguaging potential. In the next chapter, I discuss critical reinvention between communal and institutional discourses. With the potential to challenge linguistic inequality, this approach to rhetoric, writing, and professional communication can work to promote more just social structures.

6

Critical Reinvention between Communal and Institutional Discourses

THE PREVIOUS CHAPTERS EXAMINED MULTIPLE WAYS in which the rhetoric of translanguaging can be used to interrogate linguistic inequality, complicate notions of translation, and build relationships. All of these components—relationship building, complicating language ideologies, and cultivating translation spaces—promote rhetorical approaches to translanguaging. This chapter focuses on the importance of cultural components when rhetorically translanguaging, and the potential for critical reinvention between communal and institutional discourses. We have already seen a few examples of critical reinvention between the institutional discourses of medical Spanish and the patient intake forms, Dominican and US notions of Spanish, and the ways that collective approaches to interpretation can draw from a group's linguistic resources in a more beneficial way than can individual performances. In this chapter, I turn to specific examples of how the religious and cultural context of the local community in the Dominican Republic impacted a critical reinvention between institutional and communal discourses. Not only was Spanish adjusted and translated to reflect the local dialect, but certain phrasing was also added to maintain a constant presence of religious and spiritual discourse about God, control, and worldviews of participants. From individual interactions to collective action, the professional setting of medical care had to be modified to respond to spiritual needs and values of the community.

The US visitors learned that Dominican Spanish often included phrases reflecting the cultural values and worldview of the local community. A major invocation of these values lies in phrases about Dios (*God*) and notions of control in the world. In this predominantly Roman Catholic and Christian citizenry, religious phrases and notions of God are commonplace in daily Dominican discourse, especially in the rural areas. Additionally, stemming from the DR's history of colonization by Spain, the presence of Roman Catholicism entangled with the Spanish language has been deeply engrained in the discourse that travels across the country today. ¿Cómo estás? (*How are you?*) is a common Spanish phrase that second language learners are taught to ask when first meeting someone. In basic US Spanish classes, students then learn common responses to this question, such as bien (*good*), mal (*bad*), and así así (*so-so*). However, in the context of a specific Spanish-speaking country, culture, and dialect, these daily phrases may be influenced by the local communities' unique discursive practices. DR residents, especially those from rural regions, participate in everyday discourse that reference giving gracias a Dios (*thanks to God*). Thus, when speaking in the DR, instead of just answering that I am good today, I would often say, "Bien, gracias a Dios."

Although CSR's healthcare program is religiously affiliated, individuals are not required to be Catholic to participate. Even the participants who are Catholic often do not associate spirituality or religious discourse with their US medical training. However, the constant invoking of Dios in local discourses and the practice of religious prayers and songs before clinic critically reinvented the ways that we had conversations, and challenged notions of power and control. The use of various prayers, spiritual songs, and phrases asserted the agency of local volunteers within the clinic and influenced the visiting practitioners' approach to, and understanding of, healthcare while there. In *Tropic Tendencies: Rhetoric, Popular Culture, and the Anglophone Caribbean*, Kevin Browne recommends "a more practical view of Caribbean displays that rely on vernacular traditions as a means of redress, of critical (re)invention" (8). I identify religious rhetoric within the local discourse as something that reframed and reinvented the power relations of this transnational program within a Caribbean, Hispanophone context. The local community's rhetorical acts critically reinvented the visitors' notions of control, and contributed to their transcultural health education while abroad. It would be all too easy to describe this rhetoric as simply examples of religious sayings and discourse that resemble the deeply pious attitudes of rural Christian communities. But to simplify an analysis of these rhetorical acts in this way disregards their legitimacy and the agency of their rhetors.

Within the clinic in this summer healthcare program, especially following dental procedures, common expressions of gratitude included gracias a Dios y a ti (*thanks to God and to you*) and gracias a Dios por guiár tus manos (*thanks to God for guiding your hands*). In this way, patients (and sometimes parents of patients) would thank the practitioner, but only after thanking God and establishing that the procedure was successful through God guiding the practitioner's hands. This was always something that added just a bit more to the gracias that the practitioners were expecting. Not accustomed to their talents and procedures being always attributed to a higher power, the dentists seemed surprised, yet still grateful, for the expressions of gratitude from their patients. However, on further reflection, this phrasing might have seemed strange for the dental students and professionals because religion was not commonly discussed within their professional contexts of healthcare. Despite the fact that all interviewees attended Catholic institutions for either undergraduate or professional school, their cultural context of Western medicine did not often include daily discourse about God or spirituality within institutional settings. Also, because many of them were preparing to become professionals in their respective fields, they had a high regard for the authority of healthcare practitioners, and were sometimes thrown off when this authority was undercut by attributing skills and success to a greater authority figure for the patients: Dios.

When describing relationships formed with visitors, Miguel explains, "No somos iguales pero somos todos hermanos porque somos todos hijos de Dios. Entonce(s), por ejemplo, Andrés que estuvo en mi casa, yo lo trataba como mi hermano, y así lo hacemos con toda la(s) persona(s) que sea diferente (de) nosotros." (*We are not the same, but we are all brothers [and sisters] because we are all children of God. So, for example, Andrew, who was in my house, I treated him like my brother, and we do that with all the people who are different from us.*) In one way, this is a beautiful description of how to treat everyone with respect and dignity despite our differences. However, it also demonstrates the embeddedness of religiosity in everyday discourse, for Miguel explains his connection with Andrew as one of being children of God. The references to Dios were constant and spanned generations in these rural communities. Although some of the visiting participants were also religious individuals, they did not invoke God in the daily discourse in the same ways that their hosts did.

In addition to giving thanks to God after responding how you are today, phrases that were extremely prevalent included a nod toward the future and how God was the only one in control of that. Con Dios adelante was often stated when referring to how we would *move forward together with God*. Additionally, si Dios quiere (*if God wants/God willing*)[1] was the phrase that was discussed most often by the visiting participants who were previously unfamiliar with Dominican Spanish. US participants were caught most off guard when si Dios quiere was used, or added onto their sentences when saying *I'll see you tomorrow*: Nos vemos mañana, si Dios quiere. For the practitioners coming from a US cultural context, assumptions about the future and notions about having control over things were inherent in their worldview. Being future-oriented, when saying goodbye, participants would often add on that we would see each other soon or the next day. This included saying goodnight to host families. When family members said goodnight, they would often say, in Spanish, "See you tomorrow, if God wants." As their Spanish discursive interactions were consistently "interrupted" or "corrected" by this common phrase, participants began to question why the host community said it so often. Some US participants began to add this phrasing onto their sentences, while others did not. I used it as often as I could when speaking with these community members, since using it reflects how they communicate and respects their cultural values in our interactions. This phrasing has also made me question my own worldview and false notions of control over what happens in the world around me. Although I don't say, "See you next week, if God wants" in my daily discourse in English, I do not know for certain that I will see that person next week.

In my field notes during a follow-up visit on June 22, 2014, I noted an instance of this corrective move during an interaction with a couple of residents of Rancho de la Vaca. Someone had asked, "Estás viajando sola? O con otras?" (*Are you traveling on your own? Or with others?*) To which I responded, "Sola." Another resident quickly responded to correct me: "No es verdad, no estás sola. Siempre [points upward] Dios está a tu lado." (*That's not true, you are not alone. Always, God is at your side.*) This correction to the way I had answered a question might seem like a minor example, but it was just one of the many times that local residents added onto my sentences to remind me of God's presence and make my phrasing reflect their discursive tactic of adding gratitude or an invocation of Dios into conversation. Local residents hardly ever corrected my grammar, even though I'm sure I said things that may have sounded funny or incorrect in my phrasing. What seemed more important in my interactions with local residents was their reinvention of my sentences to reflect the cultural context and role of spirituality in our shared spaces of conversation.

Whether the view is of God, nature, or any other force controlling life, death, health, and human beings' paths forward, this rhetorical act forced the visiting participants to consider what assumptions are made about their own control over the world and which cultural and socioeconomic contexts promote this idea more than others. In this way, the religious rhetoric of the patients and host families altered the power dynamics in forcing a reconsideration of power and control for visitors who most often would be associated with power and control. When a visiting practitioner would say, "I'll see you tomorrow" or "We'll do that next week," the local residents would often add onto, or correct, the phrase to include "if God wants." These daily interactions were not in the control of the visitors, but were left up to a higher force. Immersing themselves in another community's local element brought up many uncontrollable forces, from multitudes of mosquitoes to new foods and language practices, so this critical reinvention of discourse was fitting for the context of our time together.

Understanding how worldview and cultural perspectives are reflected in languaging practices is important for any engagement across institutional and community contexts, but especially in healthcare. Recognizing how translanguaging gives insight into cultural values can open up possibilities for expanding our own worldviews and responses to our patients, students, or clients' needs. Taking a narrative medicine approach, Rita Charon explains, "Even though the listener thinks that all the teller gives is the facts, in fact the listener is *acted upon* by all the teller's choices—the temporal dimensions as well as other aspects of style—making the listener far more indebted to the teller's worldview and deep notions of causality and consequence than it may seem" (63). Understanding the importance of the patient's (teller's) worldview was also part of understanding his or her notions of health, illness, and purpose in life. Not only does acknowledging the influence of the teller on the listener alter the traditional power paradigm of the medical relationship, but it also investigates rhetorical acts that aim to change and reinvent the power structures that may be in place for that moment, or in the patient's experiences with healthcare.

Understanding a patient's worldview and narrative of health begins with understanding the patient's language use. Charon claims, "Our task as doctors, nurses, therapists, and ethicists is to learn each patient's personal language in its tenses, its images, its silences, and its tensions. That these narratives must unfold in time grants us the time to hear them, to provisionally understand them, and perhaps, thereby, to be of help" (67). Learning each patient's personal language will also open us up to common phrases that may be more than just a language—they may explain that patient's understanding of health and illness. As an illustration, home visits were also a part of this program, which allowed for time to listen and learn the patients' language and values. Lisa explains how these visits helped her see the benefit of caring for the whole patient: "We got to go do doctor home visits and take care of that entire person instead of just trying to fix them. So, I really think this program . . . helps people experience, not how to just fix a person and get them back to a healthy state, but to help them spiritually: talk to their family, get to know them, and do what you can and be there with that person at that moment." Lisa describes Charon's notion of being of help as one that is more than just responding to a set of illnesses. The importance of helping patients spiritually and seeing an emotional dimension to healthcare was reinforced in the daily reminder of the spiritual values the patients and fellow volunteers had. With certain participants, focusing on this spiritual dimension came from listening to their needs and being with them for a while, rather than just moving on to the next patient for the sake of time and efficiency.

COLLECTIVE PERFORMANCES OF PRAYER AND SONG

A tension arose for a number of the healthcare practitioners between efficiency and effectiveness in respecting spiritual needs at the clinic in Rancho de la Vaca. During the second summer with the program, the community leaders wanted to begin each day with announcements, a communal prayer, and a spiritual song. So I told the US volunteers that once we had the clinic materials set up for the morning, we would join the local volunteers and visitors from nearby towns in this prayer and song. The majority of the US group did not know or understand the songs and prayers, but Alexis (my assistant coordinator) and I felt it was important for us to be present with the larger group, standing in a circle with our soon-to-be patients and fellow clinic workers. US participants experienced both positive and negative feelings toward this daily song and prayer. According to the program's structure, the clinic would run only from 8:00 a.m. to 1:00 p.m. to leave the afternoons open for relaxation and time with the community. Our clinic never began right at 8:00 a.m. and, at times, the healthcare providers would not start seeing patients until 8:45 a.m. Cultural differences in concepts of time were never more pronounced than during the daily negotiation of this morning ritual and the community and providers' mutually shared desire to have as many patients seen as possible. Browne explains that

> Caribbean rhetorical performances, as a practice of judgment and a critical redress to situations that necessitate forms of display, unfold as a vernacular response to situations that come about as the result of the greatest offense—*invisibility* and *silencing*. So, to put it plainly, the fundamental motive of the Caribbean practitioner is to be recognized—to be seen and heard—in a way that capitalizes on the implied consensus of an audience familiar with his or her strategies. (3–4)

Through adding onto and correcting some of our phrasing to include Dios, and by starting our days with an emphasis on communal song and prayer, the local residents demanded recognition. They capitalized on the moments before clinics to come together in song and prayer, and to make sure that their spiritual needs were integrated in this space of healthcare. Although the US visitors did not anticipate spiritual dimensions to be included as part of the "healthcare" they would provide, the cooperadoras de salud of Rancho de la Vaca knew these needed to be included. In discussions with Miladis and Rosa, I asked if we could adjust our daily routine each week to better accommodate all of the values of our patients: being seen before the clinic closed, and starting by giving thanks to God in a prayer for everyone. The cooperadoras and healthcare team worked on starting the song and prayer earlier, but also never quite started exactly on time in a US cultural sense of the term (right at or before 8:00 a.m.).

Not everyone had negative impressions of the morning ritual. Elizabeth explains, "Every morning, we had a prayer before we opened our clinic. . . . I thought we were only going to do that for the first day of clinic. But we did it every morning and . . . it was really nice because you could see all the people still join in, and really appreciate why [the cooperadora] was there and what we were doing." This practice brought everyone together at the start of each day and demonstrated the community value of going into their healthcare consultations with a spiritual tone and a positive, communal perspective of everyone being there for similar reasons. However, it also brought up questions and concerns for the practitioners about efficiency and meeting the goal of seeing as many patients as possible before we would close in the afternoon. Seeing more patients was a value for both the local leaders and the practitioners in the clinic, and yet the issues of time and control surfaced when the clinic often would not start or finish the prayer and song until about forty minutes after the doctors and dentists were supposed to start seeing patients.

Those who struggled with this morning ritual also had questions about the purpose and quality of care. Joshua explains,

> I think we're a more time-efficient culture that like starting clinic late because of singing or prayers, you know that's just a challenge. . . . But I [also] think it's a challenge to really take each patient, kind of appreciate the symptoms and the problems with each patient because it's not about numbers, it's about helping each person. I kind of wondered if we saw forty med patients[2] in a day and some other clinics saw . . . like fifteen, did those fifteen patients get a much better experience than the forty patients we had?

Despite feeling that they could not see as many patients as they had hoped, the visiting practitioners returned to Santiago to find out that other groups had seen far fewer patients than they had. Acknowledging challenges with the religious rhetoric regarding efficiency, and also reflecting on whether efficiency was the best approach for individual patients, demonstrates the influence these rhetorical acts had on the visiting volunteers. Taking control of running a strict schedule for clinic hours and questioning each day how many patients they might see forced some participants to question their cultural logic and assumptions about healthcare and time spent with patients.

As a relatively small country with nearly 160 active Peace Corps volunteers ("Dominican Republic") as of 2017, and members of numerous nonprofit organizations visiting from other countries, the Dominican Republic is no stranger to hosting volunteers from abroad. When visiting the major cities or beaches during the summer, one will probably run into church or service groups from the United States. While spending time near the rural rivers on hot summer days, one might hear Dominicans speaking English with thick New York accents while visiting home. The Dominican Republic is a transnational space, whether migration patterns go from north to south across oceans or from east to west across the island. The island of Hispaniola hosts multiple languages and rhetorical traditions that mix and collide in ways that represent a distinctly Caribbean identity. On an island with a complex history of religion and colonization, the use of spiritual discourse in Spanish languaging to demonstrate the lack of control that these visitors have in a world guided by Dios could be seen as ironic. And yet, it can also be seen as deeply intentional for the island's current cultural climate. By integrating communal prayer and song into our workday, and by teaching the visiting group how the local discourses use invocations of Dios, the Dominican rhetors of this program reframed and reinvented the reality of how healthcare would be carried out during our time together. Though from afar it may appear as if the ones "in power" were the visiting practitioners coming to provide dental procedures and medical care, on the ground was the development of a new order of discourse guided by local residents. This new order privileged the local dialect of Dominican Spanish and community discourses of health.

Through their rhetorical acts, Dominican participants reinvented the assumed intercultural relations of transnational healthcare programs. Daily activities and language development were shaped by the community's discourse. Coming from US educational and institutional discourses on medicine and standard Spanish, the US visitors encountered very different communal discourses of rural Dominican Spanish. In the spaces where they came together inside and beyond the clinic walls, all participants in this program encountered moments of critical reinvention. This critical reinvention took place in the many translation spaces that were cultivated to introduce new words to their linguistic repertoires, nuanced perspectives on translation, and collective approaches to problem solving amid cultural differences.

During the summer of 2014, I was on a visit to check in with research participants and catch up with families I had met during the program. While finishing up a conversation with a couple that had hosted one of the medical students from my group, I explained that I had to leave for dinner but that I would be around for a few more days:

> RAQUEL: No(s) vemo(s) en marte(s). (*We'll see each other on Tuesday.*)
> MARIA (FIRMLY ADDING ONTO MY SENTENCE WITH A SMILE): Si Dios quiere. (*If God wants.*)
> RAQUEL: Sí, si Dios quiere (I repeated, embarrassed that I had forgotten to say it).

Various factors changed my planned schedule each day I was there, and it felt like I had to learn lessons all over again—that my way of speaking and viewing the world was not always right . . . because Maria and I did not end up seeing each other that Tuesday.

Conclusion: Rhetoric, Expertise, and Community Discourses of Health

I SET OUT IN THIS BOOK TO COMPLICATE PERCEPTIONS of languaging and to challenge linguistic inequalities regarding our uptake of translanguaging as a rhetorical act. My study in the Dominican Republic illuminates the potential for a rhetoric of translanguaging to complicate language ideologies, cultivate translation spaces, build relationships, and critically reinvent discourses between communities and institutions. Examining translanguaging within this specific, multilingual context allowed me to articulate how certain contexts can flip, challenge, or reinvent linguistic hierarchies. Languaging that might be considered theoretically, academically, or raciolinguistically "correct" must be interrogated to understand why people perceive it as "good" languaging, and what implications that has for how "bad" languaging is classified. We must also consider how our participation in multilingual communities and contexts would benefit from a critical understanding of language ideologies, the complex negotiations within translation spaces, and relationship building to draw from collective linguistic resources. Taking the rhetorical steps to challenge language hierarchies and to privilege marginalized ways of speaking can open up possibilities for flipping the script of what forms of languaging are most fitting for translation spaces between institutional and communal discourses.

For me, the rhetoric of translanguaging was developed somewhere between the campo and the classroom. What makes my vision for this liminal space even more apt is that the clinics we ran were located in elementary school classrooms that were converted into clinical exam rooms for the summer. The chairs and desks were used for various parts of the clinics, and rocking chairs, sheets, and other materials were brought in to set up a makeshift clinic for the month. So, in a sense, we were always in the classroom while at the clinic. However, it was not the institutional structure that defined our translanguaging potential, but rather the translation spaces that we cultivated within it. The clinical focus of our time together simply highlighted the shared goals we aimed to accomplish in providing healthcare for the community. All of the translanguaging and learning that happened with patients emerged from an intentional approach to translanguage in new ways that privileged the community discourses.

In this study, the institutional and cultural perceptions that US participants initially had of Dominican Spanish were often in relation to its variance from the "standard" medical or everyday Spanish they had learned in school. The disruptions they encountered with patients not being able to understand this type of Spanish, and favoring local ayudantes' Spanish-Spanish translation, paved the way for a new order of languaging. As notions of "correct" or "best" Spanish were redefined through interactions inside and outside of the clinics, the US participants began to develop their linguistic repertoires and draw from the collective resources of the whole group. As they worked together as a healthcare team, Dominican and US volunteers also helped each other develop their ever-evolving languaging. They used texts such as dictionaries and patient health history forms as the starting point for their conversations, and then transformed those static understandings of texts into dynamic dialogues as they asked each other questions about alternate phrasing and translation. In these ways, the local residents and their visitors cultivated translation spaces by negotiating meaning across verbal-nonverbal, written-spoken, English-Spanish, and Spanish-Spanish translanguaging. Underlying all of these moves was a constant negotiation of medical terminology through provider and patient discourses of health.

Spiritual elements in the local discourse also came into play with how local residents critically reinvented the discourse of this program to reflect their cultural values. This unique setting in which individuals from very different linguistic, economic, and cultural backgrounds lived and worked together for a month set up the conditions for great potential in the rhetoric of translanguaging by how they negotiated language variation, cultivated translation spaces, and critically reinvented discourse together. However, none of this would have been successful without all participants' intentional relationship building and persistence toward shared goals for serving the community. These components acted as driving factors in continuing to push through difficult moments of misunderstanding, cultural differences, and feelings of inadequacy in languaging ability.

As a response to the structural language ideologies of institutional discourses, the rhetoric of translanguaging illuminates the contexts and translation spaces where linguistic inequality is challenged, making room for more just social structures. Although my focus has been on a healthcare space, the implications for the rhetoric of translanguaging can be connected to any professional space that serves diverse communities with varied communicative practices. These spaces constantly struggle with differences in "professional" discourse and the discourses of patients, clients, or other stakeholders. As practitioners seek to translate meaning across differences, they may find that certain biases about languaging also play into the quality of care and services that marginalized speakers receive. This has dire implications for people's lives. If practitioners do not recognize the linguistic hierarchies at play in how they work with laypeople, they may communicate in ways that will be damaging, or demeaning, to the people they aim to serve. Therefore, self-reflexivity about language ideologies is crucial when understanding how lay terminology is discussed and perceived by professionals. When we talk about health literacy, for example, we run the risk of healthcare providers thinking that they need to bring their language "down" to the level of their patients. However, a rhetorical approach to translanguaging among Englishes, Spanishes, or any dialect and language difference, would emphasize the vast resources that patients use for discussing health and illness. This approach would recognize difference in language "not as a barrier to overcome or as a problem to manage, but as a resource for producing meaning in writing, speaking, reading, and listening" (Horner, Lu, Royster, and Trimbur 303). If the provider does not take the time to listen to and understand these ways of talking, she or he may miss major connections between the patients' worldviews and how they approach their own healthcare.

My participants encountered Spanishes and ways of communicating that created dissonance with the written resources from which they had learned "correct" language. Their classroom and cultural contexts may have led some of them to perceive the rural Dominican Spanish of their patients as bad Spanish or slang in relation to the standard Spanish they had learned in the United States. However, if participants were unable to speak this dialect of Spanish, the Dominican community members perceived them as not knowing Spanish and needing an interpreter. Despite global or academic notions of prestige and hierarchies of Spanish, this study demonstrates how the rhetoric of translanguaging can flip the script of linguistic inequality and highlight the need for privileging community discourses of health.

This notion of community discourses of health can also restructure the ways that medical providers understand lay terminology and their encounters with language variance in their work. I present "patient discourses of health" as a term that can place community terminology, phrasing, and ways of communicating on a more equal level with provider discourses of health. The languaging that patients use to discuss and understand their symptoms, diseases, and medications can provide insight into how any patient experiences health, medicine, and illness. Patient discourses of health present languaging in relation to the individual's experience and positionality as a patient. However, individuals are always a reflection of their communities, and therefore, community discourses of health represent a broader look at how groups of people (who identify as a community) communicate about health and illness in their everyday discourse together. Community discourses of health are just as rigorous and intellectual as provider discourses of health.

They reflect the intricacies of communities' experiences outside of medical settings, which are crucial to understanding what patients tell providers within medical settings. If community discourses of health are viewed with the same respect as "professional medical terminology," then notions of "expertise" in healthcare will become more holistic in their recognition of patients' experiences, environments, and social settings as being integral to understanding patients' health and creating plans for their care.

What implications might the rhetoric of translanguaging have for our study of writing and rhetoric? My hope is that we can more intentionally pursue ways to challenge linguistic inequality and make theoretical advances in how we examine and advocate for the difference within difference in translanguaging by explicitly recognizing how the interplay among dialects, written texts, oral language, and nonverbal tactics is used rhetorically in translation spaces. Examining a phenomenon like Spanish-Spanish translation can also highlight the multiple layers of dialect, accent, and technical terminology that are constantly negotiated within named languages such as English and Spanish. By giving a clear sense of how certain dialects are stigmatized over others, certain nationalities responded to with more hatred than others, and certain ways of writing considered more deviant from the standard than others, we acknowledge the importance of contextualizing and rhetorically interrogating how and why people perceive languaging in the ways that they do.

By taking a step outside our institutional contexts, we can research rhetoric and writing in new ways that challenge "deficit" models and complicate hierarchies of certain dialects over others. By examining how various social and cultural contexts privilege ways of speaking differently from the way our academic institutions do, our understanding of translanguaging will inherently grow. This is especially pertinent for scholars who have not understood the relevance or place of a translingual approach to rhetoric and writing. If we have not seen the ways that dominant discourses can be challenged and critically reinvented between institutional and communal discourses, we may consider translingual scholarship to be too theoretical or disconnected from lived experiences. My hope is that this book provides an example of how rhetorical approaches to translanguaging can promote progressive theoretical goals for the valuing of language variation while also staying rooted in the practice of individuals trying to work together to solve problems across linguistic and cultural differences.

The notion of translation spaces can highlight how groups might cultivate spaces to explore the potential for challenging these inequalities in language use and interrogating racism, classism, sexism, ableism, and other discriminatory views that place certain forms of languaging over others. We may even see classrooms as potential translation spaces where languages and modes are negotiated. However, all of this potential must be built on a foundation of relationships and trust. In translation spaces, we can build on a foundation of rhetorical familiarity and intimacy by keeping each other's common humanity and needs at the forefront of exploring translation and mutual understanding. We can cultivate spaces to ask the difficult questions about why certain ways of speaking are easier for some to understand than others, and what role institutional discourses have played in that familiarity, or lack thereof. This can also lead to critical inquiry into the interactions between institutions and communities on a broader scale. What is it about our institutional contexts that makes us deem certain discourses as fitting or appropriate over others? How do institutional languaging preferences play into the continued disenfranchisement of marginalized communities? My study begins to answer these questions by examining how standard Spanish and medical Spanish privileges certain Eurocentric ideologies about language and marginalizes communities whose speech patterns are racialized and stigmatized as deviant from the standard. However, there is much more to explore in seeking answers to these questions. By taking a step outside English-dominant settings and into this context in which a theoretically stigmatized version of Spanish was the dominant form of communication, I have tried to demonstrate ways that we can begin to break down these notions of appropriateness and flip the script on what we can imagine for translation spaces and "professional discourse."

Taking a rhetorical approach to translanguaging based on observations of interactions within a transcultural, multinational community has great potential to restructure disparate power relations and linguistic inequality. Though I admit that these are lofty goals, I believe that we can aim to accomplish them regardless of where our liminal spaces between institutions and communities may bring us to translanguage together. Rhetorical translanguaging is most effective when individuals cultivate translation spaces in response to language variation and misunderstanding. In these spaces, they can complicate perceptions of named languages, translation, and difference. By consistently working to build relationships, they will gradually trust each other more and begin to translanguage in new and innovative ways based on that rhetorical familiarity with each other. This can lead to problem solving and collective inquiry that may provide more insight than any single individual could have uncovered alone. If we encourage collective rhetorical action in our institutional discourses, we may realize the potential that translingual and translanguaging scholars have been arguing for decades: language variation is a resource and the norm of communities today. By normalizing translanguaging potential through educational institutions, we can further inform professional practices that value linguistic diversity and approach language difference as something to respond to with creativity and collective resources.

APPENDIX: INTERVIEW PROTOCOL

US Volunteer Questions

Personal Background

1. Could you tell me your name, your age, and where your permanent residence is?
2. What is your nationality?
3. What languages do you know how to speak and understand?
4. When and how have you been involved with CSR programs? Other similar programs to it?
5. Why did you decide to get involved with the CSR summer program?

Communication

1. Can you tell me about any experiences with these programs in which you could not understand what others were saying or when someone else could not understand what you were saying?
2. Can you think of any ways you communicated or connected with people without words? How did that work?
3. What was it like to hear other people speaking in Spanish or English around you?
4. Have you had any experience of someone interpreting for you or you interpreting for them? What was that like?

Cross-Cultural Communication

1. How would you describe the kinds of communication that happen between different people in these programs?
2. Can you describe a time when you learned about someone else's culture in this program?
3. Can you describe a time when you felt you taught someone else about your own culture in this program? How did you do that?

Collective Identity

1. Tell me about a time when you noticed people from different backgrounds coming together during this program. What did this look like by the end of the program?
2. How would you describe the connections people develop through this type of experience?
3. Can you describe a time when you worked with someone from a different nation or language to accomplish something in the clinic?
4. Tell me about any benefits or challenges you think come with this type of experience.

Future Programs

1. In what ways can future participants in this program prepare for communicating and working together in the clinic?
2. What do participants in the future need to know about living and working together in this program?

Additional Information

1. Is there anything else you would like to add? Is there anything you wish I would have asked?
2. Can you think of anyone I should contact who would be interested in doing an interview?

Dominican Resident Questions

Antecedentes Personales

1. ¿Podría decirme su nombre, su edad, y donde usted vive?
2. ¿Cuál es su nacionalidad?
3. ¿Qué idiomas usted sabe hablar y entender?
4. ¿Cuánto tiempo ha estado involucrado en los programas de CSR y de qué manera ha participado en el programa de verano?
5. ¿Ha tenido americanos de CSR quedando en su casa? ¿Puede describir como se ha ido esta experiencia?

Comunicación

1. ¿Puede contarme sobre cualquieras experiencias con estos programas cuando no podía entender que otras estaban diciendo o cuando alguien no pudiera entender que usted estaba diciendo?
2. ¿Puede pensar de tiempos en que comunicó con personas sin palabras? ¿Cómo funcionó esta comunicación?

Appendix: Interview Protocol / 139

3. ¿Cómo fue su experiencia a escuchar otra gente hablando en inglés alrededor de usted?
4. ¿Ha tenido una experiencia de alguien interpretando para usted o usted interpretando para él o ella? ¿Cómo fue?

Comunicación Transculturales

1. ¿Cómo descubría los tipos de comunicación que ocurren entre personas diferentes en estos programas?
2. ¿Puede describir un tiempo cuando usted aprendió algo sobre la cultura de alguien otro en este programa?
3. Puede describir un tiempo cuando se sintió como usted enseñó a alguien sobre su propia cultura en este programa? ¿Cómo lo hizo?

Identidad Colectiva

1. Cuéntame sobre un tiempo cuando podía ver gente de contextos diferentes viniendo juntos a dentro o afuera de la clínica.
   a. ¿Puede contarme sobre maneras en que usted vio la gente trabajando y compartiendo tiempo juntos en el fin del programa?
2. ¿Cómo descubriera las conexiones la gente desarrolla a dentro de este tipo de experiencia?
3. ¿Puede describir un tiempo cuando usted trabajó con alguien de una nación o idioma diferente para lograr algo en la clínica?
4. Cuéntame sobre algunos beneficios o dificultades piensa que vienen con este tipo de experiencia.

Programas Futuros

1. ¿En cuales maneras pueden preparar los participantes del futuro en este programa para comunicando y trabajando juntos en la clínica?
2. ¿Qué necesitan saber los participantes en el futuro sobre viviendo y trabajando con este programa?

Información Adicional

1. ¿Hay algo más usted quiere decir? ¿Hay algo usted esperó que yo hubiera preguntado?
2. ¿Puede pensar en alguien yo debo contactar que estará interesado en hacer una entrevista?

NOTES

Prologue

1. Some Spanish text will have the letter *s* in parentheses to denote when the speaker said the word in a way that dropped the *s* off the end, but I inserted it in parentheses to clarify what the full word was. See my translator's note for more information on these decisions.
2. Slashes in my translations represent words that could be used as an equivalent in meaning. In this case, the slash represents my unwillingness to assume I know what my three-year-old niece meant. Translating the word to "well" reflects a certain grammatical approach, while "you speak good" could also be what she meant.
3. The name of the organization has been changed.

1. Toward a Rhetoric of Translanguaging

1. According to the American Translators Association (ATA), "translation" is the written transformation of information from one language to another. Alternatively, "interpretation" is the verbal transformation of information across languages. I use both terms interchangeably to represent common discourse about translation and to identify interpretation as a communicative event that entails translation work.

2. Research Design

1. Some of the description of the study in this chapter and other descriptions of the data are similar to portions of my chapter in Meloncon and Scott's *Methodologies for the Rhetoric of Health and Medicine*.
2. All data collection and research methods were approved by the University of Kansas Human Subjects Committee (Project #20174).

3. Many local residents referred to the United States as Nueva Yor(k) (*New York*), pronouncing it in a way that often drops the letter *k*, which is where the majority of Dominican immigrants to the United States live.
4. The names of the towns and people have been changed for this study.

3. Complicating Language Ideologies

1. These characteristics were also more broadly reflective of Caribbean Spanish, but my use of "Dominican" in describing the dialect is to (1) denote the geographic location of our discursive activity and (2) reflect how my participants categorized it.
2. This normally refers to green beans, but was also used to describe black beans in a dish such as arroz con habichuelas.
3. This word has different meanings, depending on the region, but it refers to a bus or public transit van in the Caribbean. For example, in Chile, the word can signify baby.
4. This translation is from CSR's participant guidebook.
5. When I use Dominican, I do not mean that it is composed only of individuals born in the Dominican Republic of parents who are both of Dominican descent. I refer to any individual living in these communities located in the Dominican Republic.

6. Critical Reinvention between Communal and Institutional Discourses

1. For Arabic speakers, my sense is that this is very similar to the use of Inshallah in daily discourse.
2. This was an example of one of the highest numbers of patients we might see in a day, and was not an average number. It also reflected the total number of patients that were seen three at a time, each meeting separately with medical students and the physician.

TRANSLATOR'S NOTE

While analyzing the data for this project, I kept all of the transcripts with Dominican interviewees in Spanish. I translated the quotations after they had been excerpted and integrated into drafts of this write-up. Dr. José McClanahan, a trusted colleague and Spanish professor, helped look over the longer quotations in an earlier version of this text to ensure that I was translating them properly. I am also grateful to Dr. Laura Gonzales for her assistance in reviewing the text and my translations. I am extremely grateful to both of them for helping me identify areas for improvement in the readability of my translations and for ensuring that I did not erroneously translate quotations. For some translations, I have added words or made minor adjustments to phrases to improve clarity for reading them in English. As I noted in Chapter 2, I tried to make the transcripts reflect the speech habits of my participants as much as possible, and that is why many of the transcripts contain words that have the letter *s* in parentheses to indicate when it was not pronounced by the individual, but I wanted to clarify for my readers what the complete word was. Overall, I tried to maintain the integrity of the subject's original meaning and context with all translations. Finally, in interview data that is represented as a dialogue between the participant and myself, I wrote my name as what they called me; this is the reason it appears as Raquel with Dominican interviewees and Rachel with US interviewees.

WORKS CITED

Alvarez, Steven. "Translanguaging *Tareas*: Emergent Bilingual Youth as Language Brokers for Homework in Immigrant Families." *Language Arts* 91.5 (2014): 326–339. *Professional Development Collection*. Web. 27 Nov. 2017.

American Translators Association [ATA], 2017. Web. 3 Nov. 2017. www.ata net.org.

Anzaldúa, Gloria. *Borderlands/La Frontera: The New Mestiza*. 2nd ed. San Francisco: Aunt Lute, 1999. Print.

Atkinson, Dwight, Deborah Crusan, Paul Kei Matsuda, Christine Ortmeier-Hooper, Todd Ruecker, Steve Simpson, and Christine Tardy. "Clarifying the Relationship between L2 Writing and Translingual Writing: An Open Letter to Writing Studies Editors and Organization Leaders." *College English* 77.4 (2015): 383–86. Print.

Bitzer, Lloyd. "The Rhetorical Situation." *Philosophy and Rhetoric* 1.1 (1968): 1–14. Print.

Bloom, Rachel. "Negotiating Language in Transnational Health Care: Exploring Translingual Literacy through Grounded Practical Theory." *Journal of Applied Communication Research* 42.3 (2014): 268–84. *Taylor & Francis Online*. Web. 27 Nov. 2017.

Bloom-Pojar, Rachel. "Translingual Rhetorical Engagement in Transcultural Health Spaces." *Methodologies for the Rhetoric of Health and Medicine*. Ed. Lisa Meloncon and J. Blake Scott. New York: Routledge, 2018. 214–34. Print.

Bloom-Pojar, Rachel, and Laura Gonzales. "Medical Interpretation as/Is a Rhetorical Approach to Health Care." *The Rhetoric of Health and Medicine as/Is: Theories and Concepts for an Emerging Field*. Ed. Lisa Meloncon, Scott Graham, Jenell Johnson, John Lynch, and Cynthia Ryan. Columbus: Ohio State UP, Forthcoming.

Brandt, Deborah. "Sponsors of Literacy." *Literacy: A Critical Sourcebook*. Ed. Ellen Cushman, Eugene R. Kintgen, Barry M. Kroll, and Mike Rose. Boston: Bedford/St. Martin's, 2001. 555–71. Print.

Browne, Kevin Adonis. *Tropic Tendencies: Rhetoric, Popular Culture, and the Anglophone Caribbean.* Pittsburgh: U of Pittsburgh P, 2013. Print.

Bullock, Barbara E., and Almeida Jacqueline Toribio. "Kreyol Incursions into Dominican Spanish: The Perception of Haitianized Speech among Dominicans." *Bilingualism and Identity: Spanish at the Crossroads with Other Languages.* Ed. Mercedes Niño-Murcia and Jason Rothman. Philadelphia: John Benjamins, 2008: 175–98. Print.

———. "Reconsidering Dominican Spanish: Data from the Rural Cibao." *Revista Internacional de Lingüística Iberoamericana* 7.2 (14) (2009): 49–73. *JSTOR.* Web. 5 June 2016.

Bullock, Barbara E, Almeida Jacqueline Toribio, and Mark Amengual. "The Status of s in Dominican Spanish." *Lingua* 143 (2014): 20–35. *ScienceDirect.* Web. 5 June 2016.

Canagarajah, Suresh. "Codemeshing in Academic Writing: Identifying Teachable Strategies of Translanguaging." *Modern Language Journal* 95.3 (2011): 401–17. *JSTOR.* Web. 27 Nov. 2017.

———. *Translingual Practice: Global Englishes and Cosmopolitan Relations.* New York: Routledge, 2013. Print.

Charon, Rita. "Time and Ethics." *Stories Matter: The Role of Narrative in Medical Ethics.* Ed. Rita Charon and Martha Montello. New York: Routledge, 2002. 59–68. Print.

Corbin, Juliet, and Anselm Strauss. *Basics of Qualitative Research 3e: Techniques and Procedures for Developing Grounded Theory.* 3rd ed. Thousand Oaks: Sage, 2008. Print.

Craig, Robert T., and Karen Tracy. "Grounded Practical Theory: The Case of Intellectual Discussion." *Communication Theory* 5.3 (1995): 248–72. Web. 1 Sept. 2012.

Cushman, Ellen. *The Struggle and the Tools: Oral and Literate Strategies in an Inner City Community.* Albany: State U of New York P, 1998. Print.

———. "Translingual and Decolonial Approaches to Meaning Making." *College English* 78.3 (2016): 234–242. *National Council of Teachers of English.* Web. 5 June 2016.

Dawson, Robin Estrada, Jennifer F. Reynolds, and DeAnne K. Hilfinger Messias. "A Conversation Analysis of Verbal Interactions and Social Processes in Interpreter-mediated Primary Care Encounters." *Research in Nursing & Health* 38.4 (2015): 278–88. *MEDLINE.* Web. 27 Nov. 2017.

Devitt, Amy, Anis Bawarshi, and Mary Jo Reiff. "Materiality and Genre in the Study of Discourse Communities." *College English* 65.5 (2003): 541–58. *JSTOR.* Web. 5 June 2016.

"Dominican Republic." *Peace Corps.* 2017. Web. 15 Dec. 2017. www.peacecorps.gov/dominican-republic/.

El Centro para la Salud Rural [Pseudonym]. *Summer Program Guidebook.* 2011. Print.

Flores, Nelson, and Jonathan Rosa. "Undoing Appropriateness: Raciolinguistic Ideologies and Language Diversity in Education." *Harvard Educational Review* 85.2 (2015): 149–71. *Allen Press Miscellaneous.* Web. 5 June 2016.

Flower, Linda. *Community Literacy and the Rhetoric of Public Engagement.* Carbondale: Southern Illinois UP, 2008. Print.

García, Ofelia, and Naomi Kano. "Translanguaging as Process and Pedagogy: Developing the English Writing of Japanese Students in the US." *The Multilingual Turn in Languages Education: Opportunities and Challenges.* Ed. Jean Conteh and Gabriela Meier. Tonawanda: Multilingual Matters, 2014. 258–77. Print.

García, Ofelia, and Li Wei. *Translanguaging: Language, Bilingualism and Education.* New York: Palgrave Macmillan, 2014. Print.

Gilyard, Keith. "The Rhetoric of Translingualism." *College English* 78.3 (2016): 284–89. *National Council of Teachers of English.* Web. 5 June 2016.

Gonzales, Laura, and Rebecca Zantjer. "Translation as a User-Localization Practice." *Technical Communication* 62.4 (2015): 271–84. *IngentaConnect Journals.* Web. 5 June 2016.

Grabill, Jeffrey T. "On Being Useful: Rhetoric and the Work of Engagement." *The Public Work of Rhetoric: Citizen-Scholars and Civic Engagement.* Ed. John Ackerman and David Coogan. Columbia: U of South Carolina P, 2010. 193–208. Print.

———. "The Work of Rhetoric in Common Places: An Essay on Rhetorical Methodology." *JAC* 34.1-2 (2014): 247–67. Print.

Grosjean, François. "What Is Translanguaging? An Interview with Ofelia García." *Psychology Today.* 2 Mar. 2016. Psychology Today. Web. 27 Nov. 2017. www.psychologytoday.com/blog/life-bilingual/201603/what-is-translanguaging.

Guerra, Juan C. "Cultivating a Rhetorical Sensibility in the Translingual Writing Classroom." *College English* 78.3 (2016): 228–33. *National Council of Teachers of English.* Web. 27 Nov. 2017.

Heath, Shirley Brice. *Ways with Words: Language, Life, and Work in Communities and Classrooms.* New York: Cambridge UP, 1983. Print.

Horner, Bruce, Min-Zhan Lu, Jacqueline Jones Royster, and John Trimbur. "Language Difference in Writing: Toward a Translingual Approach." *College English* 73.3 (2011): 303–21. *National Council of Teachers of English.* Web. 27 Nov. 2017.

Horner, Bruce, Samantha NeCamp, and Christiane Donahue. "Toward a Multilingual Composition Scholarship: From English Only to a Translingual Norm." *CCC* 63.2 (2011): 269–99. *JSTOR.* Web. 1 Mar. 2013.

Horner, Bruce and John Trimbur. "English Only and U.S. College Composition." *CCC* 53.2 (2002): 594–630. *JSTOR.* Web. 1 Mar. 2013.

Hsieh, Elaine. "Bilingual Health Communication: Medical Interpreters' Construction of a Mediator Role." *Communicating to Manage Health and Illness.* Ed. Dale E. Brashers and Daena J. Goldsmith. New York: Routledge, 2009: 135–60. Print.

ICMN Staff. "Student Suspended for Speaking Native American Language." *Indian Country Media Network.* Feb. 8, 2012. Indian Country Today Media Network. Web. 3 Nov. 2017. indiancountrytodaymedianetwork.com/2012/02/07/student-suspended-speaking-native-american-language-96340.

Lasker, Judith N. *Hoping to Help: The Promises and Pitfalls of Global Health Volunteering.* Ithaca: Cornell UP, 2016. Print.

Leonard, Rebecca Lorimer. "Multilingual Writing as Rhetorical Attunement." College English 76.3 (2014): 227–47. JSTOR. Web. 5 June 2016.

Lindlof, Thomas R., and Bryan C. Taylor. *Qualitative Communication Research Methods.* 3rd ed. Thousand Oaks: Sage, 2011. Print.

Lu, Min-Zhan, and Bruce Horner. "Translingual Literacy and Matters of Agency." *Literacy as Translingual Practice: Between Communities and Classrooms.* Ed. Suresh Canagarajah. New York: Taylor & Francis, 2013: 26–38. Print.

Matsuda, Paul Kei. "The Lure of Translingual Writing." *PMLA* 129.3 (2014): 478–83. *Modern Language Association.* Web. 27 Nov. 2017.

Miles, Matthew B., and A. Michael Huberman. *Qualitative Data Analysis: An Expanded Sourcebook.* 2nd ed. Thousand Oaks: Sage, 1994. Print.

National Museum of the American Indian [NAMI]. "Boarding Schools: Struggling with Cultural Repression." *Native Words, Native Warriors.* National Museum of the American Indian, n.d. Web. 27 Nov. 2017. http://www.nmai.si.edu/education/codetalkers/html/chapter3.html.

Otheguy, Ricardo, Ofelia García, and Wallis Reid. "Clarifying Translanguaging and Deconstructing Named Languages: A Perspective from Linguistics." *Applied Linguistics Review* 6.3 (2015): 281–307. *De Gruyter Mouton.* Web. 5 June 2016.

Prendergast, Catherine. *Literacy and Racial Justice: The Politics of Learning after Brown v. Board of Education.* Carbondale: Southern Illinois UP, 2003. Print.

Rojas, Ricardo. "Dominican Court Ruling Renders Hundreds of Thousands Stateless." *Reuters.* 12 Oct. 2013. reuters.com. JP Morgan Distribution Services, n.d. Web. www.reuters.com/article/us-dominican-republic-citizenshipidUSBRE99B01Z20131012.

Shipka, Jody. *Toward a Composition Made Whole.* Pittsburgh: U of Pittsburgh P, 2011. Print.

Smitherman, Geneva, and Victor Villanueva, eds. *Language Diversity in the Classroom: From Intention to Practice.* Carbondale: Southern Illinois UP, 2003. Print.

Toribio, Almeida Jacqueline. "Language Variation and the Linguistic Enactment of Identity among Dominicans." *Linguistics* 38.5 (2000): 1133–59. *ScienceDirect.* Web. 5 June 2016.

Urciuoli, Bonnie. "Whose Spanish? The Tension between Linguistic Correctness and Cultural Identity." *Bilingualism and Identity: Spanish at the Crossroads with Other Languages.* Ed. Mercedes Niño-Murcia and Jason Rothman. Philadelphia: John Benjamins, 2008: 257–77. Print.

US Department of Health and Human Services. Agency for Healthcare Research and Quality, Rockville, MD [AHRQ]. "Use the Teach-Back Method: Tool #5." Content last reviewed February 2015. *Agency for Healthcare Research and Quality.* US Department of Health and Human Services, Feb. 2015. Web. 3 Nov. 2017. www.ahrq.gov/professionals/quality-patient-safety/quality-resources/tools/literacy-toolkit/healthlittoolkit2-tool5.html.

Van Engen, Jo Ann. "Short Term Missions: Are They Worth the Cost?" *The Other Side.* Jan. and Feb. 2000. Bostoncollege.org. Web. 27 Nov. 2017. http://www.bostoncollege.org/content/dam/files/centers/boisi/pdf/s091/VanEngenShortTermMissionsarticle.pdf.

Vieira, Kate. *American by Paper: How Documents Matter in Immigrant Literacy.* Minneapolis: U of Minnesota P, 2016. Print.

White, Kari, and M. Barton Laws. "Role Exchange in Medical Interpretation." *Journal of Immigrant Minority Health* 11 (2008): 482–93. *SpringerLink.* Web. 5 June 2016.

Young, Vershawn Ashanti. "'Nah, We Straight': An Argument against Code-Switching." *JAC* 29.1-2 (2009): 49–76. *JSTOR.* Web. 5 June 2016.

Young, Vershawn Ashanti, and Aja Martinez, eds. *Code-Meshing as World English: Pedagogy, Policy, Performance.* Urbana: National Council of Teachers of English, 2011. Print.

INDEX

Amengual, Mark, 48
American Spanish, 41
attunement, rhetorical, 19–22
ayudantes (helpers), function of, 32, 46

Bawarshi, Anis, 64
body language, 28–29, 82–87
Browne, Kevin, 118, 123–24
Bullock, Barbara, 44, 48, 52–53

campo Spanish, 41
Canagarajah, Suresh, 11, 12
Centro par la Salud Rural, El (CSR)
  author involvement, 5–6
  clinic hours, 123
  clinic location, 129–30
  home visits, 122–23
  prayer and song, collective performance of, 118, 123–27
  religious affiliation, 118
Centro par la Salud Rural, El (CSR), the community and
  cultural values of, reflected, 123–24, 130–31
  prayer and song, collective performance of, 118, 123–27
  pressures faced, 113
  relationship building, 90–91, 103–5
  religious and spiritual values of, incorporating, 117–25, 130–31
  sitting to connect, 103–5
  time, cultural differences in concepts of, 123–24
  translanguaging to connect, 97–105
  willingness to interact, 105–6
Centro par la Salud Rural, El (CSR), host families
  challenges faced, 112–13
  disconnects, 105–9
  familial-type identity, 90–91
  gift giving, 108–9
  power dynamics, 121
  translanguaging to connect, 97–105
Centro par la Salud Rural, El (CSR), patients
  Haitian, 52
  intake process, 64–67
  othering, language and, 52
  privileging the discourse/dialect of, 29, 40, 46
Centro par la Salud Rural, El (CSR) Spanish(es)
  categories used or encountered, 41, 46
  dissonances, 132
  learning and improving, 41–44, 46, 54–58, 68–72, 115
  mirroring, 115
  regional dialect, privileging the, 29, 40, 46, 48, 57–58, 132–33
  translation, need for, 44–45, 54–58

types used at, 41
Centro par la Salud Rural, El (CSR),
  summer healthcare teams
  ayudantes (helpers), function of,
    32, 46
  challenges faced, 113–14, 125
  collaboration/collective actions,
    109–16
  control, notions of, 118–21,
    125–26
  cooperadores de salud (health
    promoters), 31–32
  equipo de trabajo (work team), 32
  ethnic identity, responding to
    assumptions about, 50–51
  gift giving, 108–9
  Haitian, 51–52
  language abilities, assumptions
    about, 51
  languaging development, 91–97,
    130
  missed connections and
    disconnects, 115
  orientation, 41
  othering, 106–7, 115
  physical challenges for, 113
  power dynamics, 121–22
  relationship building, 70–71,
    89–99, 103–5, 110, 115
  Spanish, learning and improving,
    41–44, 46, 54–58, 68–72, 115,
    132
  Spanish, types used by, 41
  translanguaging, 44, 97–105, 115
  translation, need for, 44–45,
    54–58
  visitors, relationships formed with,
    119–20
Centro par la Salud Rural, El (CSR),
  translation spaces
  cultivating, 59–62, 82, 130
  English-Spanish interpretation,
    72–74
  nonverbal-verbal tactics, 82–87
  Spanish-Spanish interpretation,
    75–82
  written-spoken medical Spanish,
    62–71
Charon, Rita, 122–23
Cibaeño Spanish, 52
"Clarifying Translanguaging and
  Deconstructing Named
  Languages" (Otheguy, García, &
  Reid), 18
code-meshing, 20–21, 73
community, CSR and the
  cultural values of, reflected, 123–
    24, 130–31
  prayer and song, collective
    performance of, 118, 123–27
  pressures faced, 113
  relationship building, 90, 103–5
  religious and spiritual values of,
    incorporating, 117–25, 130–31
  sitting to connect, 103–5
  time, cultural differences in
    concepts of, 123–24
  translanguaging to connect,
    97–105
  willingness to interact, 105–6
cooperadores de salud (health
  promoters), 31–32
"Cultivating a Rhetorical Sensibility
  in the Translingual Writing
  Classroom" (Guerra), 20–21
cultural nod, 85–86
Cushman, Ellen, 17

differences within difference, 17
discourse, critically reinventing, 26–29
diversity, valuing linguistic, 14–17
Dominican Republic
  cooperadores de salud (health
    promoters), 31–32
  Haitian migrants, treatment of,
    51–53
  linguistic hierarchies, 46–49
  segregation in the, 51

transnational space of, 126
volunteer population, 125–26
Dominican Spanish
  characteristics of, 47–48, 68–69
  CSR teams learning, 41–44
  cultural values reflected in, 117–18
  differences in, 4–5
  incorporating to connect, 97–98
  innovative nature of, 48
  local worldview reflected in,
    117–18, 122
  race ideology and, 52–54
  religious and spiritual discourse in,
    117–23
  Roman Catholicism in, 118
  stigma in the global hierarchy, 46,
    48–50
Dominican Spanish regional dialect
  participants' integration of, 48,
    132–33
  privileging the, 29, 40, 46, 57–58,
    132–33
  stigma of, 46, 53–54
Donahue, Christiane, 30, 96

Edited American English (EAE), 13,
  15
English-Spanish interpretation, 72–74
equipo de trabajo (work team), 32
ethnic identity, language and, 49

Flores, Nelson, 15, 53

García, Ofelia, 2, 11, 17–19, 45, 49,
  63, 88–89, 91
gift giving, 108–9
Gilyard, Keith, 16, 18
God, 117–21, 126
Gonzales, Laura, 59, 61
Grabill, Jeffrey, 22, 112
gratitude, common expressions of,
  119–21
Grosjean, François, 45
Guerra, Juan, 20–21, 23

Haitian migrants, 51–53
health, community discourses of, 98,
  126, 132–33
Hispaniola, 126
Horner, Bruce, 11, 12, 30, 70, 96
host families
  challenges faced, 112–13
  disconnects, 106–8
  familial-type identity, 90–91
  gift giving, 108–9
  power dynamics, 121
  translanguaging to connect,
    97–105

idiolects, 18–19, 88–89
inequality
  challenging linquistic, 9, 23, 29,
    40, 45–46, 57, 126, 131–33
  named languages and, 19
interpretation
  ad hoc, 60–61
  defined, 141n1
  English-Spanish, 72–74
  Spanish-Spanish, 75–82
  translation vs., 61
interpretors
  language ideologies, complicating,
    24–25
  medical, 5, 60–61
  translanguaging by, 25

Kano, Naomi, 18

L2 studies, 12–14
language
  defined, 68
  diversity in, valuing as the norm,
    14–17
  embodied forms in translation
    spaces, 28–29
  ethnic identity and, 49
  gratitude, common expressions
    of, 119
  hierarchies of, 40, 46–49

nonverbal, 28–29, 82–87
race and, 49–54
standard vs. nonstandard forms, 14–17
variation, responding to, 24–25, 47
"Language Difference in Writing" (Horner et al.), 12
language education, 15–16
language ideologies
  linguistic hierarchies, 40
  rhetoric of translanguaging in complicating, 24–29, 40, 57–58
  of standardization and correctness, 46–47
"Language Variation and the Linguistic Enactment of Identity among Dominicans" (Toribio), 47
languaging
  classroom-learned vs. applied, 4–7, 68–72
  defined, 11
  perceptions, factors in, 2–3
  rhetorical analysis, elements of, 19
languaging-learner relation, 21–22
Lindlof, Thomas, 33
linguistic inequality, challenging, 9, 23, 29, 40, 45–46, 57, 126, 131–33
linguistic repertoire, defined, 18–19
literacy, translingual, 11–14
Lorimar Leonard, Rebecca, 20, 21
Lu, Min-Zhan, 11, 12, 70

Matsuda, Paul Kei, 12
medical Spanish. *See* Spanish(es), medical
medicine, narrative approach to, 122
monolingual, 12–13
multilingualism, 20
"Multilingual Writing as Rhetorical Attunement" (Lorimar Leonard), 20

named languages, 18–19, 45
NeCamp, Samantha, 30, 96
nonverbal language, 28–29
nonverbal-verbal tactics, 82–87

Otheguy, Ricardo, 2, 18–19, 49, 88–89
othering, 52, 106–7, 112, 115

patients
  Haitian, 52
  intake process, 64–67
  othering, language and, 52
  privileging the discourse/dialect of, 29, 40, 46
professional Spanish, 41

race, language and, 49–54
raciolinguistic ideologies, 15, 17, 53–54, 57–58
racism, languaging and, 17
Reid, Wallis, 2, 18–19, 49, 88–89
relationship building
  in the community, 90–91, 103–5
  rhetoric of translanguaging and, 115
  translanguaging and, 21–23, 26
rhetoric
  collective approach to, 22
  defined, 22
"The Rhetoric of Translingualism" (Gilyard), 16
rhetoric studies, 12–14, 133–34
Rosa, Jonathan, 15, 53
Royster, Jacqueline Jones, 11, 12

sensibility, rhetorical, 20
sitting to connect, 103–5
social structures, generating just, 9, 18, 131
Spanish(es). *See also* Dominican Spanish
  best vs. worst, 52–53
  categories used or encountered,

CSR, 41
el español de nosotros vs. el español de ustedes, 41–46
global hierarchical structure, 48–49
knowing, 54–58
outside the classroom, 4–7
Spanish-Spanish interpretation, 75–82
speaking without judgment, 3
Spanish(es), medical
 in the classroom, 3–4
 interpretors, 5, 60–61
 learning outside the classroom, 6–7
 participants' use of, 41
 written-spoken translation, 62–71
speaking well, meaning of, 1–2
"The Status of s in Dominican Spanish" (Bullock, Toribio, & Amengual), 48
Students' Rights to Their Own Language (SRTOL) movement, 16

Taylor, Bryan, 33
Toribio, Alemeida Jacqueline, 44, 47, 48, 52–53
transformation, translation spaces for, 9
translanguaging
 across differences, 23
 bias in, 26–27
 without boundaries, 44
 in a classroom setting, 21
 collective, 109–16, 123–27
 in communities, 14
 to connect, 97–105
 contexts encouraging, 110–11
 defined, 2, 17–18, 73
 intentionality in, 26–27
 language ideologies, complicating, 24–25
 within medical translation spaces, results of, 9
 missed connections, 105–9
 nonverbal, 99–103
 play and repetition in, 99–100
 productive, foundation for, 23
 risks in, 115
 sitting to connect, 103–5
 social interaction in, 63–64
 the standard, variation or deviance from, 14–17
 translation in, 24–25
 willingness in, 112–13
Translanguaging (García & Wei), 17–18
translanguaging, rhetorical
 critical reinvention between communal and institutional discourses, 117–27
 cultural components, importance of, 117
 developing healthcare professionals, 29
 development of, contexts encouraging, 88–89
 difference, flattening, 18
 fighting for a more holistic view of varied language practices, 29
 just social structures, generating, 18, 131
 key components, 26–29
 linguistic inequality, challenging, 9, 18, 23, 29, 40, 45–46, 57, 126, 131–33
 to promote just social structures, 9
 relationship building, role in, 88–89, 115
 religious and spiritual values, incorporating, 117–27
 rhetorical attunement and sensibilities in, 19–22
 theoretical framework for, 9–11
"Translanguaging as Process and Pedagogy" (García & Kano), 18
translanguaging study
 analysis, 36–37
 coding, 36

conclusions, 129–35
context, 10, 31–32
data collection, 32–34
interview protocol, 137–39
interviews, 34–36
later considerations, 38–39
purpose, 10, 11
research design, 30–31
transcription, 36
translation
  defined, 59, 141n1
  interpretation vs., 61
  the patient intake process, 64–67
  responding to variation, 24–25
translation moments, 61–62
translation spaces
  conclusions, 133–35
  cultivating, 25–27, 28–29, 59–62, 82, 130
  defined, 9, 25, 59
  discourse, critically reinventing, 26–29
  embodied forms of language in, 28–29
  English-Spanish interpretation, 72–74
  foundational elements, 133–34
  in healthcare, 28–29
  medical, 28–29
  negotiation in, 62
  as negotiation sites, linguistic and cultural, 28–29
  nonverbal-verbal tactics, 82–87
  participants, empowering, 115
  rhetoric of translanguaging, demonstrating, 28–29
  Spanish-Spanish interpretation, 56–57, 75–82
  study context, 61
  transformation and, 9
  translation moments in, 61–62
  written-spoken medical Spanish, 62–71
translators
  medical, 60
  patient-interpreter-provider triad, 28–29
"Translingual Literacy and Matters of Agency" (Lu & Horner), 70
Translingual Practice (Canagarajah), 12
Trimbur, John, 11, 12
Tropic Tendencies (Browne), 118

Urciuoli, Bonnie, 46–47, 62–63

Wei, Li, 11, 17–18, 63, 91
writing, translingual, 11–14
writing instruction, 15–16, 20–21
writing studies, 12–14, 133–34
written-spoken medical Spanish translation, 62–71

Zantjer, Rebecca, 59, 61

AUTHOR

Rachel Bloom-Pojar is assistant professor of rhetoric and composition in the Department of English at the University of Wisconsin-Milwaukee. Her work has been featured in the edited collection *Methodologies for the Rhetoric of Health and Medicine* (Routledge, 2018) and the *Journal of Applied Communication Research*. Rachel studies rhetoric and writing at the intersections of culture, race, language, and health, with a specific focus on transnational healthcare programs, translation practices, and Caribbean Spanish. She is interested in challenging stigma associated with language hierarchies and highlighting community expertise for rhetorical studies of language, culture, and health.

BOOKS IN THE CCCC STUDIES IN WRITING & RHETORIC SERIES

Translanguaging outside the Academy: Negotiating Rhetoric and Healthcare in the Spanish Caribbean
Rachel Bloom-Pojar

Collaborative Learning as Democratic Practice: A History
Mara Holt

Reframing the Relational: A Pedagogical Ethic for Cross-Curricular Literacy Work
Sandra L. Tarabochia

Inside the Subject: A Theory of Identity for the Study of Writing
Raúl Sánchez

Genre of Power: Police Report Writers and Readers in the Justice System
Leslie Seawright

Assembling Composition
Edited by Kathleen Blake Yancey and Stephen J. McElroy

Public Pedagogy in Composition Studies
Ashley J. Holmes

From Boys to Men: Rhetorics of Emergent American Masculinity
Leigh Ann Jones

Freedom Writing: African American Civil Rights Literacy Activism, 1955–1967
Rhea Estelle Lathan

The Desire for Literacy: Writing in the Lives of Adult Learners
Lauren Rosenberg

On Multimodality: New Media in Composition Studies
Jonathan Alexander and Jacqueline Rhodes

Toward a New Rhetoric of Difference
Stephanie L. Kerschbaum

Rhetoric of Respect: Recognizing Change at a Community Writing Center
Tiffany Rousculp

After Pedagogy: The Experience of Teaching
Paul Lynch

Redesigning Composition for Multilingual Realities
Jay Jordan

Agency in the Age of Peer Production
Quentin D. Vieregge, Kyle D. Stedman, Taylor Joy Mitchell, and Joseph M. Moxley

Remixing Composition: A History of Multimodal Writing Pedagogy
Jason Palmeri

First Semester: Graduate Students, Teaching Writing, and the Challenge of Middle Ground
Jessica Restaino

Agents of Integration: Understanding Transfer as a Rhetorical Act
Rebecca S. Nowacek

Digital Griots: African American Rhetoric in a Multimedia Age
Adam J. Banks

The Managerial Unconscious in the History of Composition Studies
Donna Strickland

Everyday Genres: Writing Assignments across the Disciplines
Mary Soliday

The Community College Writer: Exceeding Expectations
Howard Tinberg and Jean-Paul Nadeau

A Taste for Language: Literacy, Class, and English Studies
James Ray Watkins

Before Shaughnessy: Basic Writing at Yale and Harvard, 1920–1960
Kelly Ritter

Writer's Block: The Cognitive Dimension
Mike Rose

Teaching/Writing in Thirdspaces: The Studio Approach
Rhonda C. Grego and Nancy S. Thompson

Rural Literacies
Kim Donehower, Charlotte Hogg, and Eileen E. Schell

Writing with Authority: Students' Roles as Writers in Cross-National Perspective
David Foster

Whistlin' and Crowin' Women of Appalachia: Literacy Practices since College
Katherine Kelleher Sohn

Sexuality and the Politics of Ethos in the Writing Classroom
Zan Meyer Gonçalves

African American Literacies Unleashed: Vernacular English and the Composition Classroom
Arnetha F. Ball and Ted Lardner

Revisionary Rhetoric, Feminist Pedagogy, and Multigenre Texts
Julie Jung

Archives of Instruction: Nineteenth-Century Rhetorics, Readers, and Composition Books in the United States
Jean Ferguson Carr, Stephen L. Carr, and Lucille M. Schultz

Response to Reform: Composition and the Professionalization of Teaching
Margaret J. Marshall

Multiliteracies for a Digital Age
Stuart A. Selber

Personally Speaking: Experience as Evidence in Academic Discourse
Candace Spigelman

Self-Development and College Writing
Nick Tingle

Minor Re/Visions: Asian American Literacy Narratives as a Rhetoric of Citizenship
Morris Young

A Communion of Friendship: Literacy, Spiritual Practice, and Women in Recovery
Beth Daniell

Embodied Literacies: Imageword and a Poetics of Teaching
Kristie S. Fleckenstein

Language Diversity in the Classroom: From Intention to Practice
Edited by Geneva Smitherman and Victor Villanueva

Rehearsing New Roles: How College Students Develop as Writers
Lee Ann Carroll

Across Property Lines: Textual Ownership in Writing Groups
Candace Spigelman

Mutuality in the Rhetoric and Composition Classroom
David L. Wallace and Helen Rothschild Ewald

The Young Composers: Composition's Beginnings in Nineteenth-Century Schools
Lucille M. Schultz

Technology and Literacy in the Twenty-First Century: The Importance of Paying Attention
Cynthia L. Selfe

Women Writing the Academy: Audience, Authority, and Transformation
Gesa E. Kirsch

Gender Influences: Reading Student Texts
Donnalee Rubin

Something Old, Something New: College Writing Teachers and Classroom Change
Wendy Bishop

Dialogue, Dialectic, and Conversation: A Social Perspective on the Function of Writing
Gregory Clark

Audience Expectations and Teacher Demands
Robert Brooke and John Hendricks

Toward a Grammar of Passages
Richard M. Coe

Rhetoric and Reality: Writing Instruction in American Colleges, 1900–1985
James A. Berlin

Writing Groups: History, Theory, and Implications
Anne Ruggles Gere

Teaching Writing as a Second Language
Alice S. Horning

Invention as a Social Act
Karen Burke LeFevre

The Variables of Composition: Process and Product in a Business Setting
Glenn J. Broadhead and Richard C. Freed

Writing Instruction in Nineteenth-Century American Colleges
James A. Berlin

Computers & Composing: How the New Technologies Are Changing Writing
Jeanne W. Halpern and Sarah Liggett

A New Perspective on Cohesion in Expository Paragraphs
Robin Bell Markels

Evaluating College Writing Programs
Stephen P. Witte and Lester Faigley

This book was typeset in Garamond and Frutiger by Barbara Frazier.
Typefaces used on the cover include Adobe Garamond and Calibri.
The book was printed on 55-lb. Natural Offset paper
by King Printing Company, Inc.